It Starts With You

It Starts With You

Lorena Bernal

Thorsons

The information provided in this book does not constitute medical advice. Always consult with a healthcare professional before making any decisions related to your health.

Names, identifying characteristics, dialogue and details have been changed or reconstructed in order to protect people's privacy.

Thorsons
An imprint of HarperCollins*Publishers*
1 London Bridge Street
London SE1 9GF

www.harpercollins.co.uk

HarperCollins*Publishers*
Macken House, 39/40 Mayor Street Upper
Dublin 1, D01 C9W8, Ireland

First published by Thorsons 2025

1 3 5 7 9 10 8 6 4 2

© Lorena Bernal 2025

Lorena Bernal asserts the moral right to be identified as the author of this work

A catalogue record of this book is available from the British Library

ISBN 978-0-00-873325-4

Printed and bound in the UK using 100% renewable electricity at CPI Group (UK) Ltd

All rights reserved. No part of this publication may be reproduced, stored in a retrieval system, or transmitted, in any form or by any means, electronic, mechanical, photocopying, recording or otherwise, without the prior written permission of the publishers.

Without limiting the author's and publisher's exclusive rights, any unauthorised use of this publication to train generative artificial intelligence (AI) technologies is expressly prohibited. HarperCollins also exercise their rights under Article 4(3) of the Digital Single Market Directive 2019/790 and expressly reserve this publication from the text and data mining exception.

MIX
Paper | Supporting responsible forestry
FSC
www.fsc.org
FSC™ C007454

This book is produced from FSC™ certified paper and other controlled sources to ensure responsible forest management.

For more information visit: www.harpercollins.co.uk/green

'When one has the inner conviction that they could clarify the truth, it is impossible for them to hold back.'
                                             Dostoevsky

I dedicate this, my first book, to the most important men in my life. My father Enrique, my husband Mikel, my three sons Gabi, Dani and Oli, and my brother Enrique Javier. These men have contributed more than they will ever know to my finding of love, self love and love for others. Thank you for existing and for accompanying me on my life journey. I love you.

I also dedicate this to the women who gave me life and shaped me; my grandmother Nona Teresa and my mum Mirta. I have you in me and I love you.

I need to acknowledge the women that inspired this book. My special girlfriends who have accompanied me on parts of my journey and have opened their hearts to me and allowed me to open mine to them. Thank you for being there and for helping me to discover so many jewels; you know who you are.

Contents

Introduction 1

CHAPTER 1: Happiness 8

CHAPTER 2: Loneliness 26

CHAPTER 3: The Others 48

CHAPTER 4: Your Little Girl 64

CHAPTER 5: Our Script, Our Values 73

CHAPTER 6: The Game of Life 80

CHAPTER 7: The Cycle of Longing 95

CHAPTER 8: Good or Bad? 103

CHAPTER 9: Where Are You? 116

CHAPTER 10: Your Reflection 129

CHAPTER 11: Love 142

Introduction

Welcome, dear reader. I am Lorena and I can't wait to share my message with you. As well as being a mum of three, an actress and model, a life coach and spiritual life coach, the founder of the platform Live Love Better, and wearing a few other hats besides, I am a passionate student of human emotions, philosophy and spirituality. My own dream is to bring what I have learnt about happiness, love and life, through all my experiences and studies, to more people – people like you – to lead them to easy ways to take care of themselves and others, to help them find joy and peace no matter the circumstances of their lives and to honour the person they are as a whole. This book is part of that dream, and I have other big plans that I'm excited to tell you about, too. But for now, let me take your hand and guide you through the journey that I hope will be the start of a new life for you filled with love.

After all, we don't have long lives, do we? Eighty years or so is such a short time (especially if you take out the first 15, when you're not yet independent, and the last 10, when you may not be either), and it flies by! These few years are a gift, and it is so sad if we don't enjoy every moment, every person, every experience ... They are all a gift that life offers us, and I believe that's how we should take them.

Imagine our time here as a holiday that we have planned to spend in the most beautiful resort called Earth, where we will stay, if we are lucky, for about 30,000 days. Here, we enjoy, we learn, we build in some relaxation, some amazing experiences, delicious food, beautiful sights and sounds, new friends. Everyone you meet is also here on vacation and also somehow serving others in the jobs, professions or activities they have chosen. You will eventually return home, wherever that is, fulfilled and rested, having had the most amazing and enriching time. Let me tell you, this is one of the most important realisations I have come to. We have been given the gift of life on a beautiful planet; we arrive as pure, innocent bundles of love full of curiosity and excitement for this experience. It breaks my heart that we are not all happy and enjoying our time here. So what's going on?

We don't deserve to be discontent. That is not the plan. The plan is to have fun and a full, beautiful and wonderful life, to meet people and love each other, enjoy each other, share with each other and – finally – say goodbye, leaving a lot of love and taking a lot of love with us. That's it. What is the point otherwise? It's true that some of us will be exhausted at the end of the experience because we might have had an intense or challenging life, but at the end of the day, no matter how challenging the experience has been, before saying goodbye, all we will think about is the love we leave and the love we take with us. I know – and I think you may also know in your heart – that the secret to your wellbeing, to enjoying this experience of life as you deserve, to feeling happy and complete, is to find peace and learn how to LOVE, as this is at the core of our true nature. And I don't just mean how to love people, but how to love everything. The places, the smells, the sensations, the experiences, even the challenges. And, of course, how to love and care for others and also to let yourself be loved and cared for.

Introduction

You are holding the answer in your hands. Each chapter in this book will offer you insights and tools that will open your heart and help you to learn new ideas, and also help you to *unlearn* some things that have conspired to make you unhappy and unfulfilled. I am going to lead you to a place of feeling rather than a place of thinking, guiding you away from the brain and towards the heart.

My message would be the same for all human beings, regardless of gender, but here, in my first book, I have decided to be very specific. I want to speak directly to you – a girl, woman, wife, daughter, sister, mother, grandmother. You have the power to give life, to nurture, and that power carries great responsibility, because it is in your gift to pass on the message, to model that way of living, and inspire those who come next with the love that you give them, the love that they see, and the love they feel you have for them and for yourself. In your core, in every cell of your being, you have the intrinsic ability to nourish, care for and wrap others with love. The real power of women is their capacity to love. I see us as the soil around a flower, plant or enormous tree. We can inspire growth, warmth, confidence and calm in whoever is around us. So here, I want to empower women, but not to excel in business, make lots of money or be more powerful than men or anyone else. I want women to discover that their main power resides within themselves, in the love they are able to manifest and share, by doing whatever they decide to do from a place of fulfilment and wholeness.

Throughout my life, I have met many women, most of them kind and tender, full of love to give. But at the same time, many of them carry a subtle sadness, a feeling of dissatisfaction, a lack of fullness and so much insecurity and distrust. I have observed that many women lack that necessary feeling of pride and total appreciation for themselves. Most of the women I have met in my life have so much to be thankful for in material terms – or at least the essentials to feel full and enjoy and appreciate their lives – but for different reasons they don't feel complete, they can't connect with the magic they would exude if they knew the truth, if they realised the incredible potential and light they hold within themselves.

If this is you, stay with me. I have so much compassion for you, because you are beautiful and precious, and have so much to give, so much to offer, and the only thing you really need to flourish as you should is love. Surrender to love, let go and fill yourself with love – by which I mean, good love. The kind of love we think is so hard to find, because love always seems to come with conditions, and is always dependent on receiving something in return. I mean the kind of love we felt when we were little girls but someone or something took it away from us, so now we don't remember how it feels. Good love is the kind of love that we will only be able to feel if we are at peace, if we are trusting, if we are able to release the fears that lead us to judge ourselves and others and want to control everything.

These negative sensations are those that make us demand too much of ourselves, make us intolerant of imperfections, and don't allow us to appreciate the true essence that arises from within us and begs to come out and be shared with the world.

It comes down to this: in order to love others, it is absolutely necessary to have the ability to love, value and care for yourself. And if you don't know how to do this, you must discover self-love, because self-love means you have recognised the beauty of who you are and what you are, which will consequently lead you to find peace and love, and to value others as well.

Yes, it's that simple. That simple, but also that complicated and challenging.

Introduction

If you love yourself, value yourself and know yourself – properly, with good love – I promise you that many of the problems you may have, most of them likely caused by insecurity, a lack of love and a feeling of emptiness, will disappear. And only then will you finally see the preciousness of everything around you and of your interior being, enabling you to extend that love and share it with the entire world.

Unfortunately, expressions such as 'love yourself', 'value yourself' and 'know yourself' have become fashionable in recent years, to the point where they have been overused, and sometimes even misused. Few people really know their transcendent meaning. Love yourself, trust yourself, listen to yourself... I will be saying these things in this book, but I will try to explain exactly what I mean, how to do it and why it's essential to achieve it.

We will embark on this journey so that you can stop judging yourself and start to accept yourself and enjoy life, so that you are capable of feeling love without fear, so that you stop demanding from others that they fill the voids within you or give you answers. So that you can fully trust yourself and others, until your fears and doubts disappear ... In short, so that you can live in peace, calm, harmony, joy ... in love.

By sharing with you some of my experiences and what I have learnt from them, as well as real-life stories of other people like you and me who are experiencing this same adventure called life, we will together change the perspective from which we normally look at things. I will try to plant seeds in your heart so your love can flourish, and you can inspire others to let theirs flourish, too. I want to try to open your eyes to a different way of perceiving your experiences of life. To help you unlearn certain habits, certain ideas you might have that are shaping the way you look at everything, making your emotional system react in a way that you might think you can't control, or that you assumed is just part of who you are even if you don't necessarily like it. With simple words I'm going to show you that I see you, I hear you ... and with some easy, practical reflections, I will knock at the door of your awareness so that it can awaken and light up your whole world.

I am going to share with you one of the most important secrets for a full life, for making your world a happy one and enjoying every drop of experience. I'm going to try to dissect this secret into tiny parts and shine on them the light they need, so that at the end of this journey we can put all these pieces together and make perfect and balanced sense of them. My only goal is to share with you something vital and amazing, which I know at this moment in my life, having experienced, learnt and studied it a lot. This way, I feel I can contribute at least a little bit to the improvement of the world ...

You've probably heard or read this message in other books or platforms. And maybe you are still seeking answers or are even confused about what to do exactly to be released from all your concerns. My intention is not to tell you anything radically new or different, but to tell you what I've learnt in a different way, in my own way – the way only I know, because it's mine. To deliver it to you in a simple way, without detours, without too many words, without theories ... just from my truth, directly from my heart and soul. Because I know the message is simple and clear, that it is easy, but also very difficult at the same time. I write from me to you in the most direct way I know. And hopefully you will finish this book with the clarity you deserve.

We deserve to be happy, we deserve to enjoy life, to love and be loved, to value and be valued, to be appreciated, but this is

Introduction

mainly in our own hands. We don't need anything or anyone to prove to us how much we are worth or how much we can give; all we need is to believe in ourselves, to appreciate and love ourselves, and when we do this, everything else will flow and fall into place.

Even though it sounds like a utopia, a romantic dream, I believe that if we could find the Holy Grail of happiness, peace, joy and love, really, the world would be a much more beautiful environment, full of really powerful people willing to empower others instead of dominate them. We would realise that we are here temporarily and that we have come to enjoy each other and this beautiful planet. But more than that, we are here to experience ourselves as deeply and completely as possible.

You can do it, and if you don't yet know how, let me help you find the secret . . . Hopefully it will serve you, and you will finish this book with a clearer understanding of how beautiful you are and how much the world needs you, all of you, just as you are inside. With each of your flaws and each of your virtues, with each of your opinions and thoughts, your worries and curiosity, we need you. With your questions and desires, with your passions, with your intimacy and care, your smiles and tears. It's time to wake up, and, together, let's make this world as beautiful as we all deserve.

So, let's get into it, the sooner the better, for the sake of all of us and the ones to come.

Open your heart, and let me in.
With love,

Lorena

CHAPTER 1
Happiness

*'Happiness is the meaning and
the purpose of life.'*

– Aristotle

Many people in our world today have grown up with more or less the same basic ideas of who we are, what life is, how we should live it and what we are here for. I'm fascinated by the study of ancient civilisations and the ways these studies have shown that there have always been, in every era, a kind of collective unconscious belief that everyone has inside, leading them to follow the same patterns. On top of that, we have had different cultural beliefs, depending on variables like governments, resources, geographical location, climate, etc., influencing our behaviours and aspirations for life.

Each generation had a series of concepts that, without even realising it, conspired to shape their reality. According to these ideas, the supposed path to success for a female until quite recently has been as follows: be a good girl and stay silent, or at least don't be too loud. Observe and learn from the adults, and obey them, because they know better. Study and be cultured so you can work to have a future. Fall in love and marry a good man – a provider. Have kids. Be loyal to your man and make him happy. Be a good mum. Sacrifice part of the future you've worked for. Lead the home, and be there for everyone.

Happiness

There has been this idea that by following these steps, women will be happy and fulfilled and will achieve their purpose. For earlier generations of women, the path was even narrower; it was just grow up, follow orders, obey others, then marry, have kids, cook, sew, clean, nurture your children and take care of your husband.

Also, of course, they had to trust the government, respect politicians, follow the rules, and respect the royal family, the social hierarchy and the Church. Whatever the religion was, women needed to have faith, and conform to what that religion preached.

Everyone and everything has taught us these ideas for decades: our family, our schools, the books we read, the shows or movies we watch ... everything has had essentially the same message at its core, the same ideas of what a successful life experience would be. And us? Well, most of us have followed the path that has been laid out for us – what else could we do? Of course, there have always been rebels, those who wanted to do things differently and go their own way – change the course of society – but they were the minority and their voices were not often heard; they were even sometimes silenced by the majority.

Ancient civilisations and cultures lived according to different parameters: the stars, the harvests, the weather. They lived in villages full of wise elders. They worshipped many gods, they took care of the land. Life was hard and often brutal and short, but, even then, there were certainties that they believed in and followed.

But now we – modern Westerners, the supposedly developed civilisation, with these generations at the forefront of everything – find ourselves facing a very confusing reality. Do you ever get the feeling that nothing is clear right now? That everything is evolving at a dizzying speed, and that we don't really know what life is all about? That we are all in limbo, struggling to position ourselves? There are so many questions and doubts in the air right now that practically nobody knows how to fully answer them, yet at the same time we can find answers to everything, absolutely everything, at the touch of a button. The worst part is that all those answers are often contradictory. There is no clear path, there are no absolute truths, which means we now find ourselves with more information than ever, but also more doubts than ever.

If you're looking for absolute answers that will show you your future path, you are in a difficult situation. No one knows for certain whether studying will lead to success, marriage will lead to happiness, having kids will lead to fulfilment, having money will lead to abundance and satisfaction. We now have so many options, and hear so many conflicting voices, that it can feel impossible to know which path to choose and which perspectives and values to respect and trust. But let me tell you, this uncertainty, although very confusing, can also be a wonderful thing, a moment in which all possibilities are open. A moment when you can choose, when you can decide who to be and how to live in order to find your version of success, the one that resonates with you. When you can turn away from feelings of overwhelm towards feelings of empowerment. Right now, we are in a chaotic period, when many of the core systems that govern our society are being doubted – education, politics, science, economics, healthcare ... They no longer fully support us and our ideas ... It's the perfect time to create ourselves anew, to discover ourselves, to find our truths – to be an active participant in our own lives. You may not feel it yet, but you are fortunate to live in an age when you have options. You can find out for yourself what works for you and what doesn't, and where and how to find happiness, meaning and truth.

Happiness

Do we need to suffer to be happy?

The ancient Greek philosopher Aristotle wrote those words about happiness at the start of the chapter more than 2,000 years ago, but we are still not very sure what happiness is or how to find it, or even how to look for it. Our education system, our family life or society at large tells us that happiness is something that can be sought and found, that it can even be bought – it is a goal to be achieved after doing certain things. It is out there somewhere! I suspect, though, that we grow up with the feeling that it probably doesn't even exist, or, if it does, that only fleeting moments of this sought-after state are possible.

The overriding belief is that the world is difficult, complicated, that we have to struggle and fight, that to achieve good things requires a lot of effort. How many times have we heard expressions like 'work hard', 'stand up for what you want', 'you get out what you put in', 'I am a fighter'? These kinds of expressions convey that life is hard and that only those who make an effort, who 'fight' and never give up in the pursuit of happiness, will eventually achieve it. Perhaps . . .

We feel it is important for young people to work hard, to suffer, to hurt, because only then will they know what life is really all about. We feel they have to learn that sacrifices have to be made, that there are millions of obstacles in the way before they can find the truth. Because the right path is the most difficult one, and only the weak choose the easy path. We judge harshly any young person who simply enjoys life without doing anything laborious. We admire those who work and are productive and efficient, those who suffer and don't cry, those who become stronger with pain.

And, yes, many of these beliefs do have some truth to them, many of these ideas are valid, but I think it depends so much on the context. You can see life as involving pain, sacrifice or effort, or you can reframe it as an exciting adventure. There may be pain along the way, but when seen from a different angle, that doesn't have to mean you experience suffering.

When you believe there is a higher purpose within the experience that is giving you pain, you can even embrace it. I once heard it likened to giving birth. God! It's painful, and you hurt, a lot, but you don't suffer. There is pain, but there is not suffering, because you know on the other side there is a beautiful soul waiting for you to mother it. Some women even decide to feel the pain at its maximum, rejecting any medical numbness. Our life challenges come with a hidden gift, and sometimes they hurt; we just need to learn how to find that gift while we are hurting. And with that in mind, you can feel like a pencil, which would never serve its purpose if it was never sharpened.

As an immigrant myself, for example, born in Argentina into a very humble family, with a dad who started working at 15, a mum who got married at 16 and became a mother at 19, and a grandfather who fought in the Spanish Civil War and had to endure, unfairly, many years in prison before ending up in Argentina, I've always heard about how hard we all needed to work, how strong we needed to be, to have a better life in order to, I guess, be happy. I've witnessed people like us moving to different countries, working non-stop to achieve a better future for their children. This situation is very common, and the lessons are always about ignoring the pain because it's worth it, because when we get what we're looking for ... again, I guess, we will be happy.

But even in these cases, when your original situation is not your ideal, when, yes, you need to make sacrifices and work hard, and fight for opportunities, you can choose to go through the process with joy and gratitude, or with pain and suffering. If you choose the latter, I assure you, the results will never be good enough. You will always want more food for your children, a better school, better clothes, more toys, because you want them to be happy. So, will you miss out on seeing them grow up and being part of their lives just to make them happy? What if the thing that makes your children happy is having you more present, seeing you express gratitude for the experience of living, seeing you embrace your origins and your capacities, instead of resenting who you are and wanting to be constantly somewhere else in life? Sometimes children just need the basic experience of being together, all of you working on the same goal, sailing in the same boat, sharing the same dreams.

The gift is the whole process, with the joy and the pain, not the finish line.

A new way of thinking

So, how can we shift our perspective? How can we avoid being overpowered and overwhelmed by our worries? The answer is: by trusting. By trusting yourself and your choices. By making those choices from the heart, from a place of loving your life and what's to come, not fearing your life and what's to come. By being connected to your heart, and acknowledging that while being connected to its dreams you made choices, and they were the right ones, and by embracing the adventure that comes with those choices, because you have faith in yourself and your own guidance.

Think of it this way: when you take a roller-coaster ride at a theme park, you're probably scared to death, but at the same time, you're desperate to live the experience. And the steeper the loops, drops and turns, the more scared you are, but the more you want to experience it. If you trust that the car is well attached to the track, if you trust that the screws are holding everything in place and that your safety harness will hold your body well, then you will face that fear with pleasure and excitement! You might fling your arms up and yell out at the scariest moments, but you don't stop smiling and being amazed at what you are experiencing. And you know what? When the little car reaches the end of the journey, it seems like the ride was short and you regret that it is over. You might even want to get back on it immediately to feel that incredible rush again. Even if you got completely dizzy, you might feel that the experience has left you exhilarated.

I consider this a fair metaphor for life. It's tough, it has threatening loops, steep drops, even vertigo ... but if we trust in the ride, if we adopt the right attitude and mindset, we can enjoy it instead of enduring it. In fact, if we don't approach it this way, we're sure to regret it at the end when it's over, when we look back and realise that we haven't enjoyed the experience, no matter how intense it has been. And then we die and that's it, we will never ride the roller-coaster again. What a shame not to have enjoyed it; what a shame to have been afraid; what a shame not to have trusted.

The pursuit of happiness

Do you sometimes look around you and observe that nobody seems happy? Or at least not completely happy. That everyone is on the path, searching for something, involved in the struggle? Or they look busy, tired, on autopilot ... And if you know

Happiness

someone who actually shows their happiness, you think they're slightly crazy. You might even think, *Okay, yes, she looks really happy, but she's probably not showing us the reality of what's going on deep down. Not everything that glitters is gold.*

Obviously, we don't usually say this out loud – there's a kind of unwritten code of conduct in which you have to pretend that you believe the happiness that the other person is displaying. The saddest thing is that we are probably right when we don't believe that show of happiness.

It is well known now that there are people who post gorgeous photographs on their social media channels, which show them looking super-happy and enjoying life. But we all know that's not the whole picture, right? These images don't show their true reality, just an edited corner of it, and many people find these kinds of posts overdone, fake or even unbearable. Because the truth is, unfortunately, there are very few people who are at peace, who feel calm and truly happy enjoying this precious journey we call life. And I don't think those people would ever show it on social media.

Isn't this surprising? Why, as we grow up, do we see life as a problem? One great big problem made up of countless smaller sub-problems and challenges that we have to face in our day-to-day lives. And what exactly are these problems we find so insurmountable? School, university, finding a partner, clashes with friends or family, dissatisfaction with our body, finding a job, liking that job, having children, not having children, money – it goes on and on ... All these things are challenges, hurdles to jump over and problems to solve. We only stop and breathe when we are having a good time or when we are absorbed in some kind of entertainment that disconnects us from our feelings, because we feel overwhelmed, tired of trying and trying, and we need to ease that weight with activities and possessions that we desperately seek more and more of.

Beyond the shadow of this deeply rooted belief that life is tough, we are told that there is something called happiness. We get the impression that nobody really knows where it is or what it is, but if you have it or manage to find it, then you will be one of the lucky ones who will stop seeing life as a problem, and only then will you be able to enjoy it.

Yes, we will be happy, we tell ourselves, but we don't believe that anyone can really get there, and yet we keep searching, all the while not knowing what it is we're looking for. And when we do actually see it, we don't believe it is here to stay. We go through our lives suffering, sacrificing, in search of something that may not exist, convinced that it is hidden in some remote place that we can only reach after struggles and fights and stumbles and obstacles. We see happiness as a destination, an end point we want to reach, where we can finally rest and enjoy life.

What a mess.

This is how life passes us by, while we are preoccupied with wondering if happiness will arrive or not. Those who are sure it will happen believe it will only come when they have money, health, the right person by their side, when they leave the job they don't like and find the job they do like, when they start travelling the world ... And those who think happiness really doesn't exist simply learn to accept that they will never be fully happy; they'll get by with occasional moments of enjoyment.

So much has been written about these basic ideas – about how to find happiness, and what it really means to be happy. Less has been written about the mistake we make in *being sure that something doesn't exist and yet spending our lives searching for it*. If happiness doesn't really exist, then why do we waste time

Happiness

lamenting that we don't have it? Why do we waste time searching for it? And if it does exist, why do we persist in searching for it in places where we have proved, in millions of ways over the centuries, that it cannot be found?

We do know, deep down, that this is an absurd notion, yet everything about this topic confuses us and makes us feel a kind of anxiety that we mask in many unhealthy ways.

And to make matters worse, that time when we were supposed to be happy – childhood – we can barely remember; we were so innocent and inexperienced that we were unaware we were happy. It has even been suggested that we are actually *unhappy* as children but don't realise it, and that all that unhappiness remains in our subconscious and materialises in the form of trauma in adulthood. Furthermore, the theory of 'generational trauma' says that we carry the unhappiness of our ancestors in our subconscious, so we not only have our own problems to contend with, but theirs too!

So, where can we find happiness? Money? No. We know that many people with money are not happy. A stable relationship? How many stable relationships do you know that involve people who are not happy? Health? Well, it's obvious that there are a lot of healthy people who are not happy either...

I am going to show you in this book that happiness does exist, and that WE ALL know it deep down in our hearts. I believe – although the outside world insists on showing us a thousand and one times that it is impossible to reach as a permanent state – that we have a force inside us, an instinct, an intuition, a call, that drives us to search for it, and that does not let us settle in peace if we do not have it. If we really knew it was unattainable, we would stop searching and be at peace being unhappy.

Maybe the answer is that neither the concept we have of happiness, nor the places where we search for it, are right. We know how people living in the poorest and most deprived communities can really enjoy life, smile and be happy. Yet we look down on them and think it's impossible for them to be truly happy because they don't know what there is beyond their small world; we think they are happy because of their ignorance.

I tell you my friend, our concept of happiness is very, very distorted. In fact, we wouldn't actually need that disconnection we seek from our daily lives if we could really connect with ourselves, our inner peace and our inner joy at having this experience called life. Those feelings of peace and joy are there inside you, although I would say they are more than just feelings; I would call them states of being. They are there buried, waiting to be awoken and connected to you.

The happiness within

If we take a moment to think, we will realise that we have indeed had many, or at least some, moments of happiness in our lives. Everyone, regardless of who they are, where they live or how much they have, has had moments in which they were happy.

Perhaps it was when your child was born; when you were given that thing you wanted so much; when you were in nature, and you imbibed a feeling of peace and overwhelming happiness. Your wedding day; the day you sold that thing to fix your financial problems; the day you bought your house; the day you were with your friends, family or partner and enjoyed it so much.

The secret is not in what happened that day or in that moment, in what you were given or what was around you ... it

Happiness

is in who you were at that precise moment when you felt happy, what you felt inside yourself, what you had in your heart right at that moment.

Trust me, you have the ability within you to be happy, to perpetuate that feeling forever, regardless of the circumstances around you. It's in you, it's already there, waiting to shine. I will show you this in this book, layer by layer, piece by piece, so you are able to realise it and find your inner being, your true self, who is there waiting to be rediscovered. Inside you lies the key to that state of happiness that we all yearn for and have almost lost faith in, that state in which we would like to live but that scares us because we assume it will break and we will suffer again. We even sometimes prefer to stay in known suffering instead of risking the possibility of finding happiness and then losing it, or not finding it at all.

But I will tell you an absolute truth, now: in reality, *you are already happy*. Yes, you heard that right. The only hindrance is that you don't know it, you don't believe it. You have been taught to see that you are not happy. You have learned to look only at the problems, at what is missing.

You are happy, you are at peace, you are in harmony, but you don't allow yourself to realise it or open up and surrender to that state. You might even take yourself out of it when, without looking for it, you feel it. It even scares you! You feel that you don't deserve it, that it wouldn't be fair for you to feel happy given what is happening in the wider world or in your world. But know this: it's not really you that won't allow yourself to feel that happiness, it's your mind. This is what happens when we allow our heads to control us. Our brain thinks, all the time; it is wired to do that. It thinks, it compares, it expects, judges, worries, predicts, prevents ... That is what we are constantly doing when we believe we are one and the same as our thinking mind. So we feel worried, jealous, not good enough or stressed because of those thoughts.

What we need to understand instead is that we are not our minds; we are a witness to those thoughts, and that witness lives in our hearts. Our heart is pure peace and presence; the more we learn how to connect to it, to realise that is who we are, the more we will start looking at life, at others and at ourselves from a completely different perspective – from the perspective of someone calm, fulfilled and at peace. We just need to learn to stop getting drawn into the non-stop thinking that leads to the non-stop mixing of different emotions and feelings.

If at any moment we realise that we feel happy, even for a few seconds – like those moments when we peek our head out of the car window at the traffic lights and a ray of sun caresses our face; when we are under the water in the bath or the sea and let ourselves feel the silence – we often remind ourselves almost immediately of all the reasons why we are not happy. We focus on all the terrible things in our life that show us that the feeling we just had was an illusion, just our imagination, a silly dream that felt like happiness because it wasn't real. We believe that it was only in that specific moment when we let go that we were happy.

There is a simple way of summarising this in just three words (although we will go into this in more depth later), which for me encompasses everything: happiness is love. It is that clear, that simple. A deep, unconditional, overwhelming and amazing love.

What those small moments of happiness have in common is that you felt filled with love. Every pore of your skin, every cell of your body, for a moment expanded in love. When you feel the sun on your skin, you love the sun, the warmth; when you're refreshed by the sea water, you love the sea; when you're in the bath, you love the warmth of the water or the coolness, the silence, your solitude and your nudity. I'm not talking about love in a relationship or towards another person, I'm talking about loving – that feeling that makes you sigh or breathe deeply because you are love ... That love is happiness. You can even feel like crying when you are in that state, it's so intensely emotional and beautiful.

Try it for yourself, now: close your eyes for a moment, and imagine you are under the warm ocean and can feel under the water the sun's rays hitting your skin. Breathe deeply and inhale that sensation of beauty and peace. Smile, feel it ... That feeling is love; it's happiness. You are embracing the moment. Even if it's just a fleeting second of sensation, if you pay attention to it, you can connect with your truth, because that love is in you, right there. It's not that these moments create it, it's that these moments remind you that it's there within you, and they open the door for it to come out.

When you become aware of this you have the power to extend that feeling just by paying attention to it. Normally our brains are full of to-do lists, or memories kick in and make us come back from that feeling into what we call 'reality', but if whenever you feel that love/happiness inside you, you choose to observe it, not judge it, you can just immerse yourself in that state and own it, and take it with you more and more often.

What do you think? Beautiful? Revealing? Or maybe too sentimental or unrealistic? Stay with me, and allow me to try to demonstrate it to you.

Love

'Love makes the world go round', 'people do crazy things for love', 'he is a tyrant because he was always lacking love'. We have heard or said these phrases many times and that's because there is actually some truth in them. Love is a concept that hovers over everything we do, everything we are, everything we say and everything we feel. We know or intuit the vital importance of love in everything. But it's something that we see, appreciate and seek in a completely wrong way.

Yes, love is another concept that we have got completely wrong.

The problem with our concept of love is that we always try to describe it with words, using our brain to understand and explain it – these brains of ours, which judge everything, doubt everything, compare everything. And that is, I believe, a great mistake, accounting for the greatest confusion and sadness that we face throughout our lives. We don't know what love is, we don't know how to feel love, we don't know how to give love, and we don't know how to receive love.

The sentence above contains exactly the same truth if we substitute the word love for happiness. We don't know what happiness is, we don't know how to feel happiness, we don't know how to give happiness, and we don't know how to receive happiness.

We do, however, access these states of being more often than we realise. How do you feel, for example, when you come back from a trip and someone you love is waiting for you at the airport or train station, smiling from ear to ear? For a moment your heart opens; you feel love and loved. How do you feel when someone who loves you hugs you? Again, you let go and feel love. What do you feel when you've looked around for the perfect gift for someone you love, and then you see their eyes light up with excitement when they open it in front of you? I'm sure you don't stop smiling, because in that moment you are loving. What do you feel when your friends sing 'Happy Birthday' to you while smiling and staring at you, waiting impatiently for you to make a wish and blow out your candles? When someone tells you how delicious the food you prepared was? Or even when your pet comes and snuggles up close to you? You feel loved.

These beautiful interactions, filled with real connection, these glimpses of happiness and joy, are created by love – by feeling loved or feeling love for someone or something. In essence, they are the result of being in love – not with anyone or anything in particular, just being IN love. And this is what immediately makes us happy human beings. It's not that being loved depends on others; only if we allow the love within us to open up can we perceive the love we receive and only then can we truly feel loved. But, of course, these are only moments, glimpses. It's impossible to maintain them and turn them into a constant feeling. Or is it?

Reflection: Do you want to be happy?

Before you read any further, I want to ask you to think about these ideas below. I want you to realise whether or not you truly want to be happy and to be surrounded by happy people, in a happy world.

- Close your eyes for a moment and just imagine everyone being happy, everyone loving everything. What would the

It Starts With You

world be like? What would life consist of? What do you see? People shining a light of joy as they walk around, perhaps. Waiters who are happy to serve you. Families gathering surrounded by love. Schools full of happy teachers and happy students. Politicians who are calm, joyful, loving people. Neighbours who help each other. There would be no wars, on a large or small scale. Instead, there would be respect, help, kindness, joy, company, freedom, laughter and lightness.

- How is your body responding to these thoughts? Do you feel a lightness rising in you? Or do you feel sceptical, that this is impossible? Or even creepy?
- Now imagine a videogame where, instead of killing your opponents, you heal and cherish them with kisses and hugs. The goal of the game is to spread as much love and happiness as possible. When I try this thought experiment with my kids they tell me this is the cheesiest idea ever, but what if it's not?
- If you are resisting these quite radical ideas, you're not alone. If you think what I am suggesting is unrealistic, impossible or naive, that's normal. We have been conditioned to think this.
- Stay with these feelings of resistance. Ask yourself if you are more content in a world where hostile thoughts are the norm. Is it only the contrast between aggression and kindness that shows you how to value friendships and other people?
- My challenge to you as we move through this book is to catch yourself when you are observing the world from this negative standpoint. Start to shift your focus towards love and fellow feelings. At the end of each day, reflect on how this thinking is making you feel and behave.

Happiness

Remember, there is a sense in us that tells us we need challenges in order to grow, that we need resistance in order to push, that we need anger, frustration, deception and sadness in order to feel gratitude, compassion and joy. And, yes, it is true, we do need those emotions to meet with our light. But the happiness I'm talking about is not a happiness that avoids those emotions, it's a happiness that implies love for those emotions, too, because we know those are the ones that will open the door for us to feel the love we are. It's not a matter of avoiding the challenges or numbing ourselves instead of facing them, it's a matter of trusting from a deep sense of peace that we are where we need to be, in the perfect moment, and at the right place to achieve our ultimate goal, which is to be ourselves fully, open, with no walls around our hearts, no resistance, just us and our love.

If you have realised that, yes, you do want to be happy – and I mean profoundly peaceful, joyful, loving – and you want to start spreading and expanding that into the world, let's move forward, because I assure you that by resolving just a few things, this will be a piece of cake.

CHAPTER 2

Loneliness

'Solitude is not the absence of company, but the moment when our soul is free to speak to us and help us decide what to do with our life.'

– Paulo Coelho

One of the most fundamental mistakes we make is believing that in order to love or feel loved, we need someone else. A partner, family, friends, an audience, a pet . . . we need someone to love or someone to love us. But guess what? No matter how many people we have around us in those roles, we still don't feel happy. We can't be in a constant state of wellbeing in our day-to-day life, without something clouding our sensations or without disconnecting from reality via one of our many screens. We still feel weighed down by one thing or another. We still feel we need more; we think we need something different, something new, to be truly happy. We still compare ourselves to others. We still remind ourselves of everything that is missing and what is going wrong. We still magnify everything that makes us unhappy, thinking that we must change, or evolve, or do better if we really want a chance at happiness and wellbeing. And, above all, we still feel alone in this struggle, alone in the face of all the obstacles in our life.

Popular wisdom has it that happiness lies in having a community, a social environment, in feeling supported by the group, in having at least one true friend, in connecting with others. I am not going to deny that all of these things help; without a doubt, they are important, but I would like to take this thought further. I'm not talking about being okay, about getting by, about supporting each other to get through this life as comfortably as possible; I'm not talking about feeling understood or seeing that others are going through the same struggles as us, so that we feel calmer. I'm talking about being deeply happy and full; I'm talking about having the feeling that even if you have nothing and nobody, even if you're naked in the middle of a desert island, with no belongings and no company, you feel full and happy.

This state is achievable, and it's wonderful. Once you feel this way, you experience everything in life differently and you bring to the world a completely transformed version of yourself. You enjoy the company of whoever you're with, but you also enjoy solitude. Above all, you enjoy being alive, breathing and having a beating heart. But this doesn't come from any community, any friend or anything in your external environment; it is built by you, from the inside. You can get help from others, who stand there as catalysts, as mirrors, as sources of support, or even as obstacles that challenge you. But you won't feel any love from any community until you open up your own love and connect to it.

You are enough

When you reach this loving state, you won't need anything or anybody to make you better, because you'll realise that you are enough, that you don't need to be better, that you already are what you have to be, that you already have what you need and already do what you have to do.

'I do enough, I have enough, I am enough.'

This phrase marked a 'before' and 'after' for me in a particular situation. I was at a time of transition in my life – in a new city, with a new house, a new school for my children, new friendships. And I wanted everything to be perfect, as soon as possible, so that we would all be happy. And I had to do everything my way, which I was sure would work best for everyone, to make us all happy as soon as possible. This created stress inside me that I was not aware of. I demanded perfection and speed of myself, and I also demanded to be well and calm in the face of everything I had on my plate, with the sole goal of being happy. I thought that if I could get us to adapt to this new life as soon as possible, we would be happy sooner. And I also felt alone in this task of making my family happy. Then one day I found myself shouting at my son because he didn't understand something about how things were done in his new school. That night, a friend who knows me very well sent me this phrase to repeat as a mantra: 'I, Lorena, am enough, I do enough, I have enough.' The more I said it out loud, the more my eyes opened to the reality that we already had enough of everything for us to be happy. I didn't need to prove to myself or to anyone else how good a woman or mother I was, or that I was a person who could assimilate sudden changes perfectly. As I repeated it, I was filled with peace and acceptance. And from that day on, we continued to adapt to our life from another angle, by *being* happy, not *striving to be* happy.

Only when you accept that you have enough, that you are enough, that you do enough, will you find peace, because only then will you stop looking to your environment for things to improve. You will start enjoying who you are and where you are, and everything you seek will be solely for pleasure, fun, passion, entertainment, or a challenge if you want; you won't

Loneliness

be striving to become anything, because you are already everything.

It may be that you don't like where you are in life or what you do, but if you know that it's not you that has to change in your being, but rather the circumstances around you and how you face those circumstances, then, from a state of peace, you can take steps to improve the situation. When you encounter negative feelings such as insecurity, jealousy, envy or disdain, you will observe them, witness them, but you won't engage with them; they will just pass, because you will feel good about yourself. You will feel enough. If you can manage this, at least 80 per cent of your problems will go away. The rest you can change or adapt gradually.

Loneliness is one of the major causes of feeling incomplete or unfulfilled. Although we may have children, a partner, family and friends, deep down many of us still feel lonely, at risk, unsafe, fearful and alone in this world full of people where so many things happen. We feel alone in the daily struggle to reach that coveted state of happiness. It may be that we don't even aspire to be happy, we just wish we could stop suffering, stop that feeling of internal emptiness that shows itself at different times of the day, which we can't fill with anything or anyone.

Our instinct is to run away from that feeling of loneliness and emptiness, but it will inevitably catch up with us sooner or later. How many times have you felt alone? And not just alone, but misunderstood, unprotected or judged? How many times have you felt that, even though you have people who love you next to you, they don't love you enough, don't value you, hear you or see you? That nothing they give you is enough?

You feel you try to be lovable and useful, and you try hard to be a good person who is there for others, but when you have this feeling of loneliness you feel no one is there fully for you. There is a sense of distance between what you're feeling and where others can reach. And you start believing that you are not enough, that you are a victim, that no matter how hard you try they will never give you what you need, and you end up pushing others away to protect yourself. You can even end up being mean or cold, just because you're done with being good and not receiving goodness back – done with that poignant pain in your chest.

Have you ever found yourself arguing with your partner, for example, and on the inside thinking, *They don't understand. They have no idea what I'm really going through. They don't love me; if they did, they would make the effort to understand me*? Even when we see that they are making an effort to listen to us and stay present, it's not enough, because you suspect they are bored or losing track of what you are saying. And then you might say, 'I'm boring you.' Or even, 'How can trying to understand me be an effort for you? It should come from you! If it doesn't come from you, it's because you don't love me enough … at least not in the way I need. I need someone who really loves me, who is interested in what's going on inside me, who has the ability to understand me.'

Scenes like these almost always end badly. You might be crying, your partner might be angry, or perhaps you just end up feeling even more alone than when you started talking. And so you come to terms with the reality that you are alone.

This doesn't only happen with a partner; it can happen with friends, too. Sometimes, when we talk to friends, things seem different at first. If they are real friends, we will feel understood and loved, because we sense that they really want to help us, and that goes some way to relieving the sting of loneliness. But even then it's not enough, and we look for a thousand excuses to explain why what they bring us isn't enough. We think, *The one who should understand me is my partner*, or, *Since this hasn't happened to my friend, she sees it as easy. She says she loves and understands me, but in reality she has no idea what it feels like to be in my situation.* Although you can vent your emotions and enjoy moments of conversation or laughter with your friends, when you get home you realise that you still feel alone.

We may also have our parents in our lives, but even that is not enough. Often we end up thinking, *My parents really don't know me. They raised me and were the ones who knew me best when I was little. And, yes, they give unconditional love, but they don't know me ... they have no idea who I am, who I have become and what I feel inside.*

And so we're back to thinking the same thing: *I'm alone, I feel alone ... and I don't like it. I want to be loved! I want to be understood! I want to be fulfilled! For some reason I cannot feel satisfied with all that I have, and I cannot accept that this is the way it has to be. I want life to be better. I want to feel at peace. I want to surrender and rest. I'm tired.*

The lonely child

This feeling of loneliness usually starts slowly, when we are little children. Most of us can remember specific moments when we felt lonely as kids – moments when we wanted to talk and were not allowed to, because we were considered too young for our opinions or comments to be taken seriously; moments when we were hurt, perhaps very badly, and we weren't able to share it with anyone; moments when we witnessed things that made us suffer but all we could do was keep the feeling to ourselves, unable to verbalise it.

It Starts With You

When we are young, our mechanism for understanding the world is very different from when we are older. As a child, in general, we have support, or at least it seems so, from our family or someone close to us. In some ways we feel that unconditional love is holding us. Even if it's a twisted kind of love, we do feel loved and take for granted that life is like that, so we accept it and keep going. Many of us even have what we think of as a generally happy childhood.

After all, when we are born, we are just like little balls of love – the real kind; we do not know any other feeling. We are small, pure and innocent, seeing everything through the prism of the love that we are. So as we grow little by little, we start to assume that what we see of the world is how it is supposed to be, and we love it that way. We might see our parents fight; we might see adults ignore us or demand a lot from us, telling us we need to be a good daughter, a good sister, a good citizen. We might see hatred on the news. We might see adults being fake in front of each other, and we don't dare repeat what we heard our mum saying about some other person behind her back. We might see homeless people on the street; adults smoking or drinking; drivers angry at each other – and so many other things. We do not question if any of this is wrong or right – we do not have that capacity – we only witness it, absorb it and accept it, and learn to love it as we live it.

Furthermore, being those little balls of love, it is almost impossible for others not to love us in return. They look at us and they instantly become love. It is impossible not to have that feeling when you are with a baby and you feel their purity; this is an instinctive response for almost everyone. The problem starts when we grow a little older and start experiencing a world that is wrapped in fears, insecurities, demands, judgements and expectations, all on the part of the adults that we observe around us. And as we accept that reality as the norm, even though we love it because it is all we know, we start to change, we start to realise that we are separate from others, that our inner world is just ours and others cannot see it – it's just us there, alone. We realise that they can't hear us, and that what we see in them is not what they show to the outside world. We start to understand how interactions with others work. And the adults in our lives also change in front of us, as the love-filled looks they once gave us happen less and less.

The loneliness of trauma

When I was a child I experienced several terrible moments when I was deeply hurt. For example, my closest group of friends in school betrayed me in a very cruel way, so for a time I was without friends altogether. I was alone. I took refuge with my parents, who supported me in an exceptional way and helped me understand that it was not my fault but theirs, and so I made new friends, with whom I had a great time. In theory, I had overcome that experience of loneliness. But I was also alone when my father moved back to Argentina after the third time he separated from my mother . . . He departed and left me without a vital part of my life, since his presence as a father had always been tremendously strong, empowering and profound. But, due to decisions I could not yet understand, I was left without him. Again, in principle, I continued to be a happy child and adolescent, relying on my mother, my brother, my grandmother and the close family with whom I shared my life. And yet, undoubtedly, all those lonely experiences were unique to me, and I started to learn that no one else could truly understand exactly what I was going through.

When I grew up I helped women who suffered abuse as children. Unfortunately, this happens more than anyone knows, and a close relative is often the abuser, someone who – guess what? – is supposed to love you. When these women were abused they were little girls, full of love and innocence; they did not know what was going on and just felt bad, or ashamed, in those moments, and they suffered in silence, unable to share or admit what was happening to them. Even when they did reveal what was happening, often others refused to believe them or minimised the impact of what they had experienced. They learnt to hide the truth of their abuse, even accept it, and eventually bury it in the depths of their being. They accepted the world as it was, and continued to love and be loved by other family members. But that secret stayed deep within and accompanied them throughout their adolescence and into adulthood. They felt uneasy with intimacy, found it hard to trust the people who were supposed to love them, and found themselves seeking out toxic partners who confirmed their notion of what love was. The hurt and isolation that comes with these experiences goes directly to the vulnerable heart, which misunderstands love and makes you believe you are alone. The long-term harm this does is what eventually brought these people to my door seeking help.

I've seen others who experienced violence between parents as their daily bread. These children did not stop loving their parents, but instead developed a whole tangle of messy feelings inside. *Why is my loving dad hurting my mum? I know he loves her, so why does he get so aggressive with her? Why does she cry and do nothing? Is that because she loves him? Why is she so fragile? If she is weak, maybe she won't be able to take care of me. Should I stop loving my dad, or is what he is doing normal?* All these questions and more churn in their minds, and they rarely share them with anyone, growing up believing that this is how the world is, this is how love works – and even if it's not, no one else would understand. So they hide it and grow up too soon, believing that love is not a beautiful light shared by everyone, and building protections around their heart to ensure they don't get hurt. This is a lonely place to be – disconnected from your own heart, and disconnected from others.

My message is this: if things like these happened to you as a child, when you were young and your emotions were all contained inside you, they may have been resolved to a point, but they have not been removed. Your early pain may have been soothed by someone's love, or by the love you gave yourself, or simply by the presence of friends or a family member who was there to support you, like a sibling, your grandmother or aunt, but despite this support, the essence of loneliness may still have been activated in you, because you experienced emotions that you were not able to share. And so, you came to realise from a very young age that you are alone.

And this is not a bad thing; rather, I would say it is inevitable. What is *evitable*, however, is suffering from this loneliness. The moment you acknowledge this, you uncover a very big truth: you are on this journey on your own. Yes, you have people around you, but your inner journey, your true-life essence, is to be lived alone. Individually, we need to get to know ourselves, and only then will we realise who we are and who others are. In an instant, we will see that we are all truly the same and we are in this together. It might seem contradictory, but think of it this way: a droplet of water in an ocean spray would feel alone and separate from other droplets. But once it realises what it is, it will understand that it belongs to the same ocean as the others. That it is actually the ocean itself.

In the same way, we need to walk a parallel path of loneliness and solitude to realise who we are, and only then do we discover that we are all the same.

And this realisation starts with you.

The lonely adult

As adults, the way we process the world changes and the movie tells a very different story. Now we have made sure our hearts are well protected so no one can hurt us any more. We tend to lose that trusting openness we once had, closing all the doors to our love and to our true self. We approach life using our loyal brains, which have recorded all the details of our past experiences to keep us safe. When things happen to us, when we're facing difficulties, external or internal, we are no longer present; we lose ourselves along the way, and it becomes very difficult to find real support, because the one who was loving us unconditionally was our own heart, and that heart is now hidden and silenced. Even if you have someone in your life offering you external support, their comfort is usually not enough to resolve the deep loneliness you feel. As an adult there is no cushioning love surrounding us. That has melted and faded away, so everything goes directly to the dark, anguishing void.

We are no longer children, and so we perceive this suffering differently through the expectations we have built up throughout our lives. We have somehow learnt that love is conditional, transactional. *I love you because ... and you love me if I ...* That pure, unconditional love that was in our hearts as children has gone, giving space to a love that we rationalise. We explain it with words, rather than just feeling it as a state of being. We have expectations for ourselves and for others, for life; we have

Loneliness

logic; we have boundaries; we have all these words in our head to retell every single story of our lives. We perceive reality through those stories we tell ourselves and we react to that reality. We no longer love and accept the present moment without expecting something in return. We don't even allow ourselves to release the pain we feel, as we don't cry loudly any more, we don't move and jump and shout; instead, we try to control and hold in every reaction. We are managed by our head, no longer by our heart.

So that leaves a permanent hole, an emptiness inside us, which is dark and makes us feel a silent and almost imperceptible anguish in the depths of our chest. So, what do we do? We spend our lives looking for people or experiences to fill that void of loneliness, that lack of love that we feel, which we can't embrace, accept or face.

We look for romantic relationships with people we immediately find things in common with, to convince ourselves that, yes, this is the ideal, this is the one, they will complete me and make me happy. Or we do all we can to look super-gorgeous, spending time and money on clothes, make-up, beauty treatments ... whatever it takes to make us feel beautiful and like we are taking care of ourselves, to mask what we feel inside. Or we work like crazy, allowing ourselves no free time and repeating the mantra: 'I am a super-productive, hardworking, amazing woman.' We might also take enormous pleasure and comfort in eating things we know aren't good for us but that make us feel good, or those little treats we indulge in every night, like drinking, to relax. Or we focus on being super-mothers, super-lovers or super-friends to make us feel accomplished, full and complete. Of course, often we are doing all this, looking for fulfilment, without even realising it.

That feeling of loneliness and unease accompanies us wherever we go – sometimes silent, sometimes invisible, but it's always there. We push it away by various means and so we think we are solving it, but we are not; we are just numbing it. It's time to face the truth and fix it so we can say goodbye to this sensation. Let's understand what it is, and solve it.

The key to paradise

It's true that at times we feel happy and very comfortable with life and with ourselves, but then, why do we feel disgusted with ourselves after eating or drinking too much, or when we realise we are using certain habits that we know damage us? Why do we overreact as soon as someone triggers us? Why do we get irrationally angry and irritated when our children don't do what we expect? Why do we have big arguments with our partners, parents or siblings? Why do we judge that friend behind their back? Why do we complain about work? In other words, why is it that the things we use to soothe our loneliness, and which, in principle, make us happy, also make us feel bad as soon as the situation becomes a little skewed or doesn't meet our expectations?

Isn't it strange that the things that help us carry on with our lives make us hate ourselves for doing them, and the people we cherish and need the most, the ones who love us the most, are the ones who ignite our greatest frustrations?

Why do I seek refuge in my parents, because they understand me, but then get excessively irritated when they are not my idea of 'good parents'? Why do I feel excessively sad when my partner does or doesn't do something that is important to me, even though I am happy to have them as my partner? Why do I panic when I see my child not behaving as they should and

I have to face the possibility that they will deviate from the path that I have carefully curated for them, to help them be successful and happy, even though they make me feel fulfilled and complete? How can it be that the ones I love the most are the ones I can 'hate' the most?

I'll tell you why this happens. Because nothing and nobody, no matter how much you or they try, will ever completely eradicate your loneliness and suffering. They will always be there, buried deep within your soul. Relationships and activities may cover it up, and you will strive to make that happen, but as soon as they stop working as you need them to, you will find yourself facing the terrifying fear of the emptiness within you ... unless you address it, unless you find a way to solve it, and unless you realise that only you have the key to that enormous door that would immediately transport you to paradise. No one and nothing else can give you this key; only you can.

The process

Oh, those moments when we actually discover the loneliness and lack of love hiding inside us! That's when our mind starts saying, *It can't be ... I have everything*, or, *I have almost everything I could possibly need to be happy! And there are many people who are much worse off than me. Why do I feel this way? What's wrong with me?* These thoughts lead to anger – and, so, you know what? You decide not to go there, not to feel that feeling. You blame your imagination, your hormones, your period, the menopause for these thoughts. You tell yourself you're exaggerating. You turn away, press the snooze button, hide the feeling even deeper than it was before, if possible, and you strengthen that inner shield behind which your greatest fears are kept until it feels unbreakable. You do this because it allows you to live, as well as you can.

I've just summarised in a few words a process that almost all of us go through once, or maybe a thousand times, a day. It's a process that has become automatic, habitual; it's one we carry out on an emotional level almost without realising it. It happens in an instant, in milliseconds, without thought.

It's very similar to what happens when we feel happiness and our head reminds us of all the reasons why we feel bad, but in this case we feel bad and our head reminds us how unfair or disconcerting that is – and, of course, it hides that feeling as best it can behind the shield we have built up. Because just as the feeling of happiness scares us, since we can lose it at any moment, the empty feeling of loneliness makes us panic, and under no circumstances are we willing to face it, especially as we can bury it so easily.

What's the problem with this system, then? Some will say, 'It's fine, I'm getting by like this, I'm enjoying the good moments and avoiding the bad ones.' At first glance, this approach seems like it could work, but you and I know that it doesn't. We know that no matter how hard we try, this attitude towards life only serves to feed our discomfort. We don't enjoy life to the fullest. Even when we're in places we like to be, we're not completely present, enjoying the moment. Not at the kids' school performances, not at a dinner or nightclub with friends, not at a family gathering or a romantic dinner with our partner; we're not fully happy, because we can't consistently connect with a feeling of wellbeing – not even in a spa while we're getting a massage!

We seek happiness like robots on autopilot, asking others to make us feel good. We keep up this continuous search for the impossible because (I'm sorry to say) with that shield in place, it is completely impossible to be happy and live in love and peace.

Loneliness

We built that shield around our heart, very carefully, piece by piece, as we grew up. Every time we get hurt, we build another piece, and every time we perceive the possibility of hurt in the future, we reinforce it. The pure, open heart with which we were born gets covered over and protected little by little so we don't feel the acute pain when it is wounded. And, sadly, it gets wounded very often, especially when we're young and vulnerable, so we end up covering it completely, allowing no access to it whatsoever. All our emotions, expressed and received, are stopped by that wall, so that it's just not possible for them to reach our hearts. And so we go on with our lives, unaware that no one, not even ourselves, can truly touch us. There is no way we can love and feel loved properly with that protection around our beautiful heart.

You will always relate to others from this safe side of the shield. Your conversations, your curiosities, your pleasures – everything will come just up to the point where your armour begins, but that armour is strong; it will block out whatever comes from the outside.

Yes, you have a great time when you do sports, when you read, when you talk to loved ones, when you're going about your daily life, or at work or with your partner – you enjoy your life while there is 'noise' around you. But nothing, no one, not a single sound can penetrate that armour you have built around your heart, and which day by day you are strengthening ... not even yourself. And if you don't dare peek at what is behind that shield, you will leave infinite aspects of yourself unknown and unexplored.

You fear the extreme vulnerability that you would expose if that barrier were broken; you feel you would be left raw and completely open to pain, and under no circumstances will you let your life break. You've worked really hard at being well, you've worked really hard to make the effort each day to take care of yourself and those around you, to be a good person, good friend, good wife, good mother, good daughter, good lover, good human being. So why on earth would you allow yourself to open up and expose all your wounds and vulnerability to the world? It would be madness. And besides, you don't have the time, desire or energy to face that ... It's such a dark, unknown place, so why would you go there if you're not certain you'd be able to get out again?

It's funny, because I don't think many of us know what being vulnerable truly feels like. We tend to associate the concept with fragility, being breakable, and we don't want that; we want to be strong. But neither our concept of vulnerability nor our concept of strength are exactly right. To be vulnerable means to open the heart completely, so that it's exposed to the possibility of harm. And to be strong means to be vulnerable but so firm in your own presence that you know nothing will ever have the capacity to alter who you are. So, if you have the strength and courage to open the walls protecting your heart, you will become vulnerable yes, but you will stand strong, unwavering and firm, and face the world as yourself. It is extremely scary and quite hard to achieve if we get immersed in the relentless flow of our lives. Maybe we can get a glimpse of that feeling when we are sick and we have no option other than to let go of control, and suddenly we realise that other people are willing to take care of us and cuddle us, and it feels good ... so good ... but as soon as we feel better, we go back to thinking in terms of 'strong' or 'fragile' – always working on being 'strong' – while in the meantime we put back that amazing shield we've built, and continue with our lives, not looking back.

Maybe we have noticed all this in ourselves and so we seek help by going to therapy. And maybe in those moments during therapy or coaching sessions we will dare to open up and reveal the truth. We might cry, vent, understand, plan to make changes to feel better. But that's as far as we get if we don't address what we have discovered, if we don't do the work of bringing up what we've learnt in our day-to-day life. It may have felt quite revealing while we were in the sessions – we may well feel lighter, but we can sometimes make the mistake of using that lightness to go back to our normal life, making no changes, but with a renewed energy, so we can keep going for some time until we feel the need to go back to a therapy session to decompress.

Therapy is an amazing way to pause the hamster wheel of life, reflect and start observing your own patterns of behaviour. It can also help you wake up to the immensity of the universe that lives inside your heart. But it relies on you to take that awareness and explore that universe in every moment of your daily life. Otherwise, even the best therapist or coach will not be able to help you break the habit of approaching life with your shield up. Keeping that shield in place means only using your mind, your logic and your memories to process your emotions, instead of your heart, your love and your magic. If you don't do all the work that therapy requires of you, you will probably still feel better, and relieved, and it can help you in certain areas ... but the whole process of healing and revealing what's inside depends on you.

Conflict

So here we are, that's how we live, day after day, night after night, until there is a moment of high emotional intensity – a conflict, for example – when you are no longer able to keep your cool.

When you enter the emotional hurricane of any conflict that may arise, you may find that you don't know how to address your inner turmoil, because it turns out that the tools you need are trapped behind that armour you are not willing to let go of. You are caught in the storm of your feelings, wanting to get out, but you are on your own, feeling all the pain that has built up inside you, alone, with no idea of how to get out of there, and you are dragged along by tears, anger, hatred, rage, resentment, envy or jealousy. You need to resolve it, so you desperately ask for help from whoever is closest to you – your partner, for example. But what if, just at that moment, they happen to not be available? They might be busy with something of their own, or they might try to help you but don't understand what you're going through. Or they might get caught up in that emotional hurricane, too, and can't come close to helping you resolve your issue. And so we're back to the same sensation of loneliness, the same thought loop: *This person doesn't satisfy me, because they are unable to help me when I'm feeling bad. They should understand me, they should know me, they should calm me ... but they don't hear me. They ignore me. They're not smart enough, or mature enough. They don't know what they need to know about life.* So, it's their fault, you think; it's their responsibility to help you feel better, one way or another. Not to mention the fact that we might see them as the cause of our internal conflict in the first place.

If you don't have a partner, you might want to use whoever is closest to you. There is a pull towards *I just need to feel loved to sooth this emotion*, and so you might silently cry for help, perhaps from your children, your parents, your friends ... or you might expect something else to help you instantly feel better: working longer hours, eating, shopping, alcohol, tobacco, medication or screens – anything that can make this storm stop!

I wouldn't recommend indulging in these things that might at first seem to make you feel better, as what they're doing in reality

Loneliness

is numbing you or disconnecting you from your emotions. However, asking for help from the people around you is essential as the first step to uncovering your heart. When you feel this way, often the last thing you want to do is ask someone to help you, as you assume that if they love you, they should be doing that without you asking. Maybe you are ashamed of your feelings, or cannot even verbalise what's going on inside you, so that asking for help ends up sounding more like an attack. As neuropsychologist Russell Barkley once said, 'The people who need the most love ask for it in the most unloving ways.' You might want love from your children, but you ask for it by shouting and complaining because they don't talk to you or kiss you any more, or you might get angry with your parents because they don't listen to you. The thing is that you are experiencing a storm of conflicted feelings inside you, which you cannot solve yourself. You sense that only love will sooth it, but no one is loving you the way you need it, so you feel alone and get even more upset.

Use these moments! Resist the urge to numb yourself or disconnect, or feel sorry for yourself. Take a breath to calm the anger, frustration and disappointment you're feeling in your body. Instead of focusing on the other person's reactions or words, observe yourself. Where is all this rage coming from? Where are you feeling it? It is a blessing to have people you can express all of this to, because just the fact of having them there is helping you get to know yourself better. Instead of judging their reaction, or their ability to see you or hear you, use them as a mirror to look at yourself and your actions. Are you overreacting to something? Are you scared? Are your expectations too high? If so, why?

Once you have calmed down, try not to blame others. This is the time to start figuring out how those emotional storms have been created inside you. The tools you need to resolve any conflict are within you, but to access them you will first have to break down that barrier you have built around you to be able to live your life, but before that you need to look at it and realise that it's there. And we are not usually in the habit of looking in there. We use our time to look outwards, because nobody has taught us how to look inwards.

Reflection: Who are you?

It's not easy to look inside yourself when you're not used to it, but it's the only way to stop blaming others and going to them for love and attention. We are very used to judging others – we know exactly how to describe their qualities and flaws. But what about you? Are you able to describe yourself? Do you know yourself? In this reflection, let's try to recognise some of your inner qualities. For example, are you shy and introverted? Do you speak to strangers easily, or are you more of an observer? Are you a warm, kind person? If so, are you like that all the time, or only with certain people? Are you different with your parents and with the rest of the world? Are you aggressive, impulsive, a follower or a people pleaser? Do you say 'yes' to everything even though it could work against you, or do you mostly say 'no' because you are always unsure? Write a list on a piece of paper, just for fun.

Remember that these qualities are not you; they are not traits that are written in stone in your DNA. They are simply ways of behaving that you have developed from the circumstances you

Loneliness

have experienced in your life. What we're trying to do here is shift the angle from which we look at things and find the source in us. It's the first step to seeing yourself, discovering yourself, and eventually finding out that there is a being in you waiting to be acknowledged. Hopefully, you will realise that she's there always, with you, for you, and that you are not alone.

Now go back over your list and pick out a couple of qualities that you don't really like, or that you feel are not really serving who you truly are, or are damaging you in some way.

Go back in time and try to remember when you were not like that. Maybe you need to go way back to memories of when you were three or four years old. My guess is that you will realise that you were actually a very sensitive and loving child, with a giant, shiny heart.

The final prompt is to try to remember what happened from then on that led you to develop these qualities that you don't appreciate in yourself.

I would like you to realise that it is because of your life's circumstances that, in order to cope and survive, you had to build the kind of personality that you now think describes who you are.

This little reflective exercise can open a window for you to see that your true being is hidden somewhere deep inside you, and that you buried it because you felt you needed to be someone else in order to be loved, to be with other people, to not be alone.

Think about how life would be if we could find the tools of self-discovery and emotional healing, and embrace the liberation that arises when we surrender our need to control this life. How would life be if we faced our inner struggles – the ones that have been there for a long time – with courage and authenticity, without fearing being alone in the process?

The tools to discover your true and unique essence are within your grasp.

CHAPTER 3
The Others

'What the wise wants is found in himself; what the vulgar wants is found in others.'

– Confucius

What does it mean to lose yourself? It means forgetting to look inward and only looking outward. It means waiting for everything to be resolved from the outside and assuming you need things or people to help you be happy. It means assuming that all causes and solutions are outside of you. That you have to learn from the outside, observe from the outside, analyse from the outside, integrate from the outside.

It means not looking inside yourself, not stopping and being aware of your profound inner world and only functioning from the perspective of the external world.

Let me show you some real case studies exemplifying how this can show up in our lives and the impact it has.

Maria

Maria has been married for 15 years. From the outside, it looks as if she has a happy, almost perfect marriage. She is beautiful and very capable; her husband is attractive and has

The Others

achieved great professional and financial success. They go to parties, gatherings and social events and nothing outwardly gives away the inner torment that Maria is experiencing. Her husband has a daughter whom he loves from a previous relationship and Maria feels that he always prioritises his daughter over her. He likes to go out with his friends, and she feels that he also prioritises them over her. He comes home tired from work and never sits with her and wants to know how her day was or how she feels. She loves him, and knows that he loves her, too, but she is very unhappy because this man does not make her happy. He does not make space for her in his life. He does not seem to really care about her. Everything else seems to be more important to him than her – or at least that is how she feels.

She doesn't know what to do, or how to act. Too many demons are undermining the relationship, and Maria can no longer take it. She has explained to her husband a thousand times, in tears, that she is not happy and why; she has told him again and again that this cannot continue and that she will leave him ... but she never does. And then, when it seems as if she is just about to take that leap and go, he comes to her, crying and apologising, telling her that she is right, he will change. He asks for her forgiveness, says that he loves her very much and that he will do everything possible to make her happy because she is the most important thing in his life, and that he is an idiot for not making her feel that way. This sense of finally feeling valued and loved fills the void for Maria, and so she forgives him ... until a situation arises that brings the demons back to the surface and the pattern repeats. This has been the dynamic of their relationship for 15 years.

Adela

Adela, who has been with her husband for 20 years, also has an apparently happy marriage. They are the centre of a large family, always great hosts and an example to follow for others. However, Adela is tremendously unhappy, and only when she is alone does she dare face up to how unhappy she is. She compares herself to other people and feels guilty for being unhappy, because she has a good marriage in many ways: they have money, health, two wonderful children ... 'I can't complain,' she tells herself, but when she opens up, she explains the reason for her misery. She has caught her husband several times sending messages to other women. When she confronts him, he cries and asks for forgiveness and promises that he will not do it again because he truly loves her. He assures her that his flirtations with other women mean nothing and that he's an idiot to risk losing her.

'How can it be that I give everything to him, and he keeps on being unfaithful to me over and over again?' Adela asks herself. 'I don't deserve this! This is not the kind of husband I want. I deserve something better. I deserve to be happy.' Yet there she remains, after almost 20 years of what must feel like torture.

It's not about judging the husbands in these scenarios, though we might be tempted. What I want to dig into here is that these women are not happy. And if they are not happy, why don't they change their situation? And if they decide they don't want to change their situation, why can't they be happy? Why do they feel trapped, powerless, fragile, fearful – even addicted – to these situations that make them so unhappy?

These women are extremely unhappy and, apparently, they can see the cause of that unhappiness: their husbands. They believe that what would make them happy is their husbands loving them truly. So they are judging their emotions and feelings on what they are experiencing in the outside world. If only they would take the time to look inside themselves and ask, 'Why am I with a person who clearly doesn't love me the way I need? Why don't I have the courage to leave and search for happiness? Why do I keep forgiving him when I know he will hurt me again? Where does this need for him come from?'

They know they should do something about it – they are intelligent and aware – but they also know there would be some emotional digging to do in order to make their life better, and they don't dare go there. They blame their husbands, and they keep on living that way. But how could they start digging in a way that feels bearable?

Another angle of analysis

The first layer of analysis would be to explore the mind and its memories, question any lessons these women might have learnt, and probe any thoughts, fears and worries they might have. They might ponder some big questions: *Maybe I am repeating a pattern that I'm used to and somehow this feels like home. Or maybe I've learnt that as a woman I have to be of service to others and put others' happiness before mine. Maybe I'm scared of being alone; I'd rather take his company and protection and enjoy the good moments instead of being on my own carrying the weight of life.* There are several different possibilities as to the reasons why these women stay in those relationships.

However, I'm not here to judge or analyse anyone; I'm here to try to open a door to another angle of analysis, which is the heart. As we discussed earlier, most people live with their hearts covered, hidden, unreachable, and this leaves them unable to feel real love. The cerebral mind is not capable of feeling love so it will always try to rationalise it and apply logic to it. But love is a state on its own; it's not something to be understood. When you are in a state of love, the first person you touch with that love is yourself. You love yourself and recognise that you deserve only love, respect and peace. If we were able to do this, we would organically move away from a relationship that did not surround us with that. Then that love in us would expand and touch anyone we are with. Loving others this way means accepting them, not trying to change them to suit our needs or change the way they live to comply with our rules of life. We may suggest some changes if we see that what they are doing doesn't serve their purpose, but if we do this from a place of authentic love, we will respect and accept their path, their ways, their pace and their decisions, knowing that our happiness shouldn't rely on them doing what we think is right. When you are in touch with your heart, you know how worthy you are, and you can dare to give your whole self to anyone who can accompany you on your path.

The tricky thing here is that sometimes it's only when we are struggling in any kind of relationship that we can start to see what is going on inside us. We might need someone to squeeze us to see what we exude. Sometimes, we need to go through situations that push us to our limits in order to realise our truth. It can be challenging and painful, but if we work on discovering and unveiling ourselves above all, we will face whatever challenges arise from a place of strength. Of course, we need to work on the relationships that are causing us pain – whether they be with a partner, siblings, friends or in-laws – and set up boundaries, as well as talk, communicate and forgive. But the job will never be completed unless at the same time, on our own, with ourselves, in our silence, we also look inside, and act from what we unveil. In other words, if a relationship is causing us pain and all we do is work on the relationship, we will never find all the truth of that pain. We need to use that struggle to figure out how we love, what we need, what we lack, our patterns, our demands ... Eventually we just need to get to the point of realising that all that pain could be erased by us allowing our love to awaken and expand. We just need to let it shine through. Let's look at some other cases that can show us how we often deal with others and the outside world.

Carla, Juana, Ursula and Natalia

Carla is divorced. She lives alone and seems happy; everything is going well. She claims she doesn't need anyone, and feels glad she no longer has a partner she ends up fighting with or having to give explanations to. But when she gets home and sees herself alone she collapses. She can't sleep without pills and can't stay asleep unless the television or radio is on. If she wakes up in the middle of the night, she needs to eat to assuage her anxiety and turns the television back on to fall asleep again. She used to blame her ex for feeling this way, but she has no one else to blame any more.

Juana can't find a partner. She actively goes on dates with several people she meets online, but they always 'turn out to be frogs'. She finds herself arguing with many of them and even ends up crying. She thinks they all have quirks and none of them are what she needs. *Where am I going wrong?* she wonders. She dresses very well, goes to the gym, eats healthily, is an entrepreneur . . . but she doesn't have any luck in love and, at 38, she feels as though the clock is ticking. 'It's so hard to fall in love with someone!' she says. And she blames her single status on the other people not being good enough.

Ursula is happily married without children. She has a wife and a great job, but she seems to have no time for anything. She's always in a hurry, always busy being successful. She exercises frantically, eats whatever is put in front of her, and is full of anxiety and stress. Never, ever calm, she feels as though life is passing her by at a thousand miles an hour. She tells people she is super-happy and complete, but deep down she knows she is missing out on life by not allowing herself to stop and feel who she really is.

Natalia is 36 years old, a beautiful and talented woman who also doesn't have any luck with love. She's had some serious relationships, but she is someone who wants to connect with her partner on a very deep level, diving into discussions on important life issues very early on. Making these quick, deep connections often leads her to move in with the partner, talk about getting married and having children. But then what happens? There always comes a moment, sooner or later, when she feels they are not deep enough to understand her. She understands them, even mothers them, but they never fully live up to her ideal of the protective and understanding father figure she is seeking. In the end, she leaves them, loving them a lot, but always thinking, *No, they weren't the one. Surely the right one is out there waiting for me?*

I have deliberately chosen cases of women who outwardly seem to have everything, and whom you might assume were very happy. I wanted to present examples of real women, in real

The Others

situations, who cannot be happy, who cannot take steps to move away from their unhappiness, despite apparently having every advantage of wealth, health and success.

These women feel something lacking inside, but again, they don't look there. They search outside for what it is they feel they are missing; they look for a partner, they work on their appearance, they turn to food or entertainment for fulfilment ...

They might be able to acknowledge a direct cause of their unhappiness – maybe a past trauma or a formative experience – or they might not know where this unease comes from, but either way, they are stuck in this state because they don't have the tools to take the lead and change their situation. It seems as if they are powerless in the face of real life, even if they try hard to heal and to fight for happiness.

Believe me, we all have the power to change our life, all of us, but the tools are inside us. Truly. We just need to learn how to look for them there.

The main tools to make changes and create the life we really want are confidence and peace. Confidence comes from removing our insecurities, and rewiring our habit of comparing ourselves to others or to our ideal self. It comes from being aware that you once knew you were special and whole, but other people's words or actions made you think you actually weren't that important. Becoming aware of this is the big first step towards recognising your own worth and your own light.

Peace comes from surrendering. From no longer blindly chasing your ideals, no longer escaping from your darkness or resisting the struggles. From accepting your situation, trusting your path and reaching that state of love. There is nothing to be scared of, absolutely nothing. Wherever you are in your life is the exact place where you need to be to challenge your acceptance, your trust and your love.

The more you dare to sit in silence with yourself, the more you will start listening to your inner voice and trusting what it has to say. Only then can you start to see the way out of your predicament and the way forward towards the life your heart wants – not your mind, with all the confusing information it has inside it, but your heart. It's your heart that knows why you are here, what you want from life and what you can give to the world.

To be able to connect with your heart, you need to pause and let go of thinking that you always need to keep moving forward. I always say, 'The Earth will still rotate no matter what you do or don't do.' So try to be just in silence as much as you can, sitting with yourself, asking questions. Allow yourself the space to hear the answers. Just breathe . . . be . . . and surrender. Let go of looking for happiness and fulfilment in others and what they can give you. They will never be perfect, they will never be enough, until you start looking for the answers within yourself.

My story

I have gone through several situations in my life that were similar to some of these women's experiences. Things have occasionally happened that have made me open my eyes and change my focus, representing a turning point in my growth as a person. By making these changes, little by little, to turn my gaze inwards towards my inner world, my emotional system has learned, adapted and evolved into what it is today.

I'll tell you about one of those turning points, which happened to me a few years ago and could help present a possible alternative way of looking at a situation involving another person that is making you unhappy.

The Others

One night I was in the living room of our house, watching a movie with my boyfriend. I had been preparing a work upgrade for months that would represent a radical change in my life, a tremendous professional leap that I really wanted to make and that I had prepared long and hard for. I was at a point where I only needed to take one more step to make it happen – a step that did not depend on me, but a kind of sponsor; all I needed was a signature from one particular man, which would allow me to start. I had done everything in my power for months, put in a lot of effort and devoted a lot of time and energy, to get where I had got to. I had sent the sponsor a couple of emails explaining that I only needed his approval, his signature, in order to move forward and that, please, I needed it as soon as possible, because if he said no for some reason, I did not have another person like him who met the necessary requirements for that step. He did not answer my first email, nor the second one I sent after waiting a couple of weeks. And so there I was, a couple of months later, watching a movie quietly with my boyfriend in the living room of our house.

It was around 10 p.m. when my phone rang. 'How strange – who would call at this time?' we said. We paused the movie. I looked at my phone screen and it was him! It was the man who could finally advance my career as I wanted, who could validate all my efforts ... He was calling me, finally! I told my boyfriend, 'It's him! I'm so nervous, look – my hand is shaking. I'm going to the office to talk. Oh my God, please, please, say yes.'

My boyfriend said, 'Good luck!' and I went to the next room to take the call.

After at least half an hour of conversation, I hung up. The sponsor had said yes! He was going to sign the document that would enable me to take that tremendous step. I couldn't believe it! I was happy, relieved, thrilled. I left the office dying to share the incredible news with my boyfriend...

When I entered the living room, however, I immediately saw that he had changed the channel and was watching a football game, and he was completely focused on what he was seeing. He saw me enter the room but was still looking at the game. I sat down next to him, silent, as he continued to watch the game, his gaze fixed on the screen. I waited for a few minutes – or seconds, I don't know; they seemed eternal – and then, finally, with my blood boiling, my stomach and heart shrinking, I asked him, trying to contain my anger and disbelief, 'Are you really not going to ask me what he said?' He knew what that call meant to me. He had seen me work towards that moment and had supposedly listened to me every time I'd said, with hope in my heart, 'I need this so badly.'

As soon as I angrily asked him the question, he stopped watching the game and almost jumped, saying, 'Yes, of course! How was it? What did he say?'

Do you think I answered him? Of course not. I said, 'Oh, now you're interested, now you're asking? How can it not be the first thing you ask as soon as I walk in the door? How can you have forgotten? How can you not care?!'

To which he, surprised, said, 'Of course I care. Come on, what did he say?'

Still full of pride, anger and sadness, I replied, 'I don't feel like telling you now.'

'Why don't you want to tell me? Come on, tell me what he said,' he replied.

'Why are you pretending? It's clear that you don't care,' I snapped. 'It's impossible to forget about something that matters to you. I was in the next room for half an hour on a call that you know meant everything to me, and you weren't nervous, alert or anything ... You started watching a football game and forgot! I can't believe it.'

He then started getting offended and said, 'How can you say that I don't care? How can something that is so important to you not matter to me? Can't you understand that I got distracted? Just tell me what he said and that's it.'

Thus began a long and intense discussion, in which I ended up crying, he ended up angry, and everything went wrong.

In the heat of the moment, a whole avalanche of thoughts, feelings and emotions came upon me. I was deeply hurt by his indifference, because it felt like he didn't love me. It seemed to me impossible that someone could love me and not find important what was important to me, or even be unaware of how important something was to me.

I went out of the room crying, going over in my mind what had happened, and every time I told myself the story I expanded it and combined it with other past moments when he had also 'shown' me that he didn't care about me and that he really didn't love me. I couldn't stop convincing myself that our relationship was no good, and that I needed someone who really loved me.

Now, let's just step back a moment. I had just received the call I had so long been waiting for. I had been given the best news I could get because it finally meant that all the possibilities I had worked so hard for would open up for me ... and yet I was giving more importance to the fact that my boyfriend had not immediately asked me how the call went. There I was, lying on the bed, in a sea of tears, when something wonderful had just happened to me! And, of course, it wasn't that he hadn't asked me; it was the fact that he hadn't asked me at the moment when I expected or thought he should have.

The next morning, we were still angry – or at least I was still angry. He tried to pretend that nothing had happened, but I turned away when he came to say goodbye with a kiss before going to work. I stayed at home, alone, all day. And, already calmer, this is when I realised several things.

I kept thinking about his reactions. First, how he had reacted the moment he realised he had been distracted. He had immediately showed an interest in my call. Why would he pretend to care if he didn't? Maybe he wasn't pretending ... And if he was pretending to care even when he didn't, maybe it was because he cared about me ...

Then I thought about why he got so offended and angry when I shouted at him that he didn't love me and that he should stop lying to me. I realised it was because I was really hurting him by saying all those things. The truth was that he had shown me a million times that he loved me, that I was the love of his life, so why did I doubt it? What had happened to me? What would have happened if, when I walked into the living room, instead of waiting for him to ask me, I had happily said, 'He said yes!' In that case, he would have jumped up, hugged me and congratulated me.

Why did I test him like that? Why did I wait for him to ask me about the call? Why did realising he'd changed the channel while waiting for me make me doubt his interest in me? Why was I not sure of his love?

So I started to realise that maybe the problem was with me. It seemed terrible to me that he had changed the channel while I went to talk in the office, that he hadn't immediately asked me how it went when I came back to the living room. He had been distracted for a moment because he was focused on the football game, and it had slipped his mind ... It hadn't been a big deal for him, but for me, it had meant that he didn't love me, I didn't matter and I needed to be with someone else.

And then there I was the next day telling myself that I was wrong, that my boyfriend did love me. I remembered all the moments when he had been by my side. I was literally having a conversation with myself, as if one version of me was trying to heal and make my other self see that I was wrong, that I had internal issues that had absolutely nothing to do with him. Something had to change. So this time, I didn't let my wounded self take over. This time, I was open and listened to my true self – the one without wounds, the one that knew peace and truth. Of course, it was ridiculous that what had happened the night before had completely erased my happiness at my great news, that I had focused solely on suffering from a supposed lack of love from my boyfriend. Is that normal? Well, friend, maybe it *is* normal, but it's definitely not healthy.

Has this ever happened to you? Have you ever felt unloved by someone who was supposed to love you, whether it was something big or small, leaving you feeling deeply sad? If so, Houston, we have a problem that we need to solve, and we *will* solve it.

Reflection: Looking at ourselves before others

Unless we are experiencing abuse in our relationship and are in genuine danger, we must look at what is happening to us with clarity and objectivity and acknowledge that perhaps, before anything else, we need to examine ourselves and take responsibility for our own issues – not because any hurt caused to us is our fault, but because we deserve to find the tools and the power to make the changes we deserve in our life.

No one decides when they are little that they are going to be causing or receiving pain. The life we haven't been able to control has made it this way, but now we can decide to observe, use and change whatever we feel if it is not aligned with our truth.

Try to identify a negative emotion in you that is linked to someone else – anger, frustration, envy, resentment ... anything you feel that is caused by that person and is disappointing you. It might be your partner, your parents, siblings, friends, in-laws ...

Sit on what happened for a minute, visualise them saying what they said, or doing what they did, or any circumstance that they caused.

Now, instead of focusing your attention on them, pull that attention back to you, to your chest. Go to where the emotion you're feeling is being born. What do you feel? Is it sadness? Is it fear?

You might say, *Well, yes, I feel sadness, but it's because they did ... and said ...* Whatever you want to say to justify or erase it, pause and just focus on your sadness or fear. Sit there and explore your feelings. You might say to yourself, *I'm sad because I want them to love me. I'm scared that they will leave me. I'm sad because they don't respect me, because they don't value me ...*

You'll probably find that it's much easier to sit in anger or resentment than it is to sit in sadness or fear ... It's much easier to focus on blame, on what the other did, than on our sorrow. Because it hurts!

Last of all, feel that sadness and think, *Am I feeling this because of what they did/didn't do? Or is it because they are not behaving how I expect, or how I think they should? And, if so, where do my*

The Others

expectations come from? Why do I think they should behave in a certain way and not how they are choosing to behave? Why can't I just accept that this is the way they want to do things? You might think, *Because it's not fair. Because I don't deserve it. Because I'm trying my best!* But if you have all these answers so clear in your mind, why are you suffering? Why do you need what you need from them? Why do you need them to change whatever they're doing?

With this reflection, I want you to dig into yourself, to find the source of your emotions. It might be that you are overreacting because you have been hurt before and you don't want that experience to be repeated, or you might find that you are scared or feeling insecure ... Or you might just find that they are in the wrong and that's it, but in that case, you might need to realise that holding on to those negative feelings towards them won't change them; it will only drive you further away from peace.

Use all this to find yourself, to connect with your truth. We want to erase our ego, our stubbornness, our expectations, and know ourselves, so we can honour who we truly are, while allowing other people to have minor faults and flaws just like our own.

Only when we have truly met ourselves and recognised that person within will we have enough clarity to judge accurately the behaviour of others. Only then will we be able to look at what others are doing and decide what we want to do in response – whether we want to stay or leave; whether we want to keep numbing our real emotions with unhealthy behaviours or find that willingness within ourselves to make changes.

CHAPTER 4
Your Little Girl

'We have to listen to the child that we once were, the child who exists inside us. That child understands about magical moments.'

– Paulo Coelho

I am not here to lecture you from a medical, scientific, biological or neurological standpoint, because I am not a doctor, scientist, biologist or neurologist, although I have studied and learned from many. I also do not want to speak to you from a psychological or psychiatric perspective. I want to talk to you person to person, woman to woman, from soul to soul.

Our childhood shapes us, builds us and defines us in an unmistakable way. What we experience as children stays with us always; it is marked on every cell of our being. We may have experienced things in our own flesh, at vital moments in our childhood, when we were learning what love is, which have given us a warped impression of that wonderful state.

As little girls, we are pure love, pure heart; in fact, the logical brain hardly acts at all – we are vulnerable, pure and precious. If we experience violence, abuse, shouting, neglect or abandonment, we take in wounding messages about who we are and how much we deserve to be loved. We learn that someone who loves us can hurt us, and that we cannot trust someone we admire or love.

These experiences can leave a small child in complete confusion, because for them, love is unconditional, beautiful, pure, and suddenly they are confronted with the opposite. As children, we might see our parents suffer or hurt each other, we might see that one of them does not listen to us or take our opinion into account, or that they laugh at us. We learn that in some way, someone we love and who loves us can hurt us. We do not understand it. What we do instead is record that the pain we feel is linked to love; that insecurity, doubts, mistrust, disappointment and wounds are all linked to love.

All this mixes with our purity and goodness because at that age we do not know how to be any different. We are beautiful; we like to draw, paint, dance and play. We like to be hugged, to be kissed. We laugh. We float through life, emanating a precious and bright light, and we open our eyes wide when we look around us. And, at the same time, we might be going through experiences that confuse us or shake us completely. It is shocking how fragile and vulnerable we are to the outside world and how much damage these situations we experience or witness can do to us.

If there is any positive aspect to all this, it is that in that moment, at that young age, we do not realise what is happening to us, that something is wrong; it simply happens to us and we accept it. The problems come later, when we apply those confusing lessons of childhood to our adult relationships with others and with ourselves. It wouldn't be such a big problem if, as soon as something bothers us, we realised that it was somehow linked to our childhood experiences, enabling us to set out to address it. But most of us integrate these feelings into our identity, and so that way of being and expressing (or not expressing) emotions becomes an intrinsic part of us, and the more time passes, the more difficult and painful it is to heal.

Mixed messages

Even if you haven't experienced anything tragic or traumatic in your childhood directly, you're not completely exempt from this confusion, as the societal model in which we've been educated gives us mixed messages about what true love is, how we should love others, how we should let ourselves be loved and who deserves to be loved.

We grow up knowing that killing is bad, but then we have to praise the people who have defended our country by killing others. We have fun playing videogames where the goal is to kill. It's acceptable to smoke when we know that 'smoking kills' . . .

We grow up knowing that everyone has value, but of course we also observe that value depends on race, gender, physical appearance, social class or success. Inevitably, it confuses us to see such differences in how people are valued.

We're told we shouldn't be selfish, that we should be generous, but we're also told we should take care of ourselves. Yet if we think too much about ourselves, we're criticised for being egocentric. We should have humility and not boast about our successes, but, at the same time, society tells us that we have to value ourselves. Wear make-up and dress well, but don't feel too pretty, because then you're conceited. Know your worth, but make sure you hide it – don't think you can go around talking about it, especially if you're a woman.

These constant messages we receive from the outside world are so contradictory! So when we become adults and can choose what to do and what to think for ourselves, and forge our own opinions, it's no surprise that we're not clear about anything. We don't really know what love is – how we should love ourselves, how we're supposed to be loved, how we should love others, what's right or wrong, what the limits are or what's acceptable and what's not.

All we can do is respond as best we can to what crosses our path in the outside world. And it works this way not only in love, but in anything. We see or experience something and judge it, and based on that judgement, we decide whether we agree or disagree with it, and which approach seems right to us. And that's how we form our internal blueprint of what, how, when, with whom. And we follow this blueprint in any situation, any opinion or response we take, any step or reaction towards a moment, person or feeling; we keep our loyalty to that internal structure we formed. But this blueprint, in the end, is not us. We don't truly believe it, because we haven't created it ourselves. It's a reflection of our subjective opinion of the realities we observe day to day, and not necessarily our true values. It's not something we've decided based on who we are, it's something we've decided based on what we see out in the world and how we respond to it.

It's almost imperceptible, but you can notice yourself doing this. Think, for example, how many times you have wanted to do something that comes from the heart, but first you have passed the idea through the thought filters of: *Will it be well received? Has it been done before? Will others like it? Will I be shooting myself in the foot? Will it harm me? Will they think I'm foolish? Is it too cheesy?* It's very rare to see completely spontaneous actions in relationships. Every response, action or decision we come up with is either based on, or filtered by, what we've learnt from our familial and societal experiences.

Does this resonate with you? As adults, it's almost impossible to recognise our true selves if we don't take the opportunity to ask ourselves what we want, how we want it or even, simply, who we are. If only we could erase all the patterns and ideas we've learnt over our lifetime and go back to feeling as authentic as we felt when we were children.

Healing old wounds

As mentioned earlier, childhood shapes our sense of security, our self-esteem and our needs; this is when our internal guide to how relationships work is formed. So, when we become adults and face a situation in which we are with someone who is supposed to love us deeply (according to our internal guide), but then they do something that is not part of our 'guide to being a good lover/friend', or they don't do something that is included in our guide, we feel destroyed. They take us to that place of feeling unloved, exposing those childhood wounds that we carry, which fill us with uncertainty about who we are and how much we are worth. They take us to a space where we are small, vulnerable and confused. And, of course, we blame that person for making us feel this way.

'I blame my mother because she doesn't love me like a mother is supposed to and makes me feel abandoned ...' 'I blame my husband because he doesn't know how to love me. I need someone who makes me feel safe, protected, understood.' This is how we carry on, blaming others for how they make us feel, and this is how our train of thought goes on and on.

And you know what? It's not them. In fact, we ought to thank them, because their behaviour shows us the mess that we have inside us. They can open the door for us to see what's in there. And when we go through that door and get there, to that emotional place, that's when it really hurts.

I'm not saying that what others do or don't do is right or good, but I am saying that if we can fix that inner turmoil that they ignite in us, we are then equipped to face whatever happens to us from a different perspective, from a place of peace and calm, without adding past stories to the present situation, so that we can just simply face the situation for what it is. Consequently, we can make decisions based on the situation itself, not on our history.

Imagine it like this: you have an open wound on your arm and someone brushes past you, accidentally touching the wound. It hurts, a lot. But it's not the fact that the person touched you that hurts, it's the fact that they brushed against that open wound. You might not even have known that you had it, or can't remember where you got it. But you've had it for such a long time that it might even be getting infected and spreading to other parts of your body, which could then become much more sensitive than normal. If this happens to you, you have three options: you can blame the person who touched you for causing you intense pain; you can realise that you actually have an open wound and start to remember where you sustained it; or you can recognise your wound and start healing it without going over how and when you got it. This third way might even allow you to thank the person who touched you, because they have helped you locate the wound that was eventually going to fester and make you sick, if it hasn't done so already, enabling you to begin the healing process.

If we can achieve this kind of understanding in relation to our emotional injuries, we won't react from the wounded place we inhabited as a child; instead, we will act in accordance with what is happening to us at that moment. We will be much more faithful to reality and fairer to whoever is with us, and we will feel strong and secure in any decision we make, because we will make it without the emotional burden of those painful wounds.

It Starts With You

To do this, however, we need to be willing to accept that the cause of the pain might be within us. We might not know what or who wounded us and, honestly, it doesn't really matter at this point. It's not about blaming or hating ourselves for having these wounds, it's about daring to stop blaming others and facing the fact that we are human and might therefore have damaged areas we need to heal. It seems simple, but you can't imagine how hard it is to recognise your own unique wounds. None of it is your fault, but that doesn't mean you don't have to take the lead now and make the decision to recognise, accept and heal your hurt. In the end, this will help you uncover once and for all your true self, all shiny, clean, bright, unashamed and joyful.

The trouble is, we don't know how to process our pain any other way. We develop an outer shell, forged from the wounds of our childhood experiences, and we blame others when they touch those tender spots. My mother did it the same way, and my grandmother, and my friends – no one has taught us to do it any differently. We've always acted this way, and we've always seen others act this way. We even see it in movies, in novels, in everyday life. It is a habit, and we assume there is no other way, telling ourselves and others: 'I am who I am because of everything that has happened to me, and this is just how it is. If you like it, great, and if you don't like it, I'll find someone else who knows how to handle me, who truly understands me, who fulfils me.' But how difficult it is to find someone who can do that. How difficult it is to be with someone for a long time and not end up separating or leading independent lives because of our own individual unhealed wounds.

Often, we don't have the time or the willingness to use our already flagging energy to work on all this. So instead, we just tell ourselves that true love doesn't really exist, right? That's it. Real, enduring, unconditional love is a lie, and one that harms us, because it makes us search for an ideal that doesn't exist. It is just normal to suffer in love, right?

And so we continue trying to explain what's happening, trying to justify it, and convincing ourselves that in reality, complete happiness, inner peace and calm – combined with pure, unconditional love – do not exist. Which is sad, because as little girls we may have experienced true love inside us, but we perhaps hold onto that memory as a mere illusion, which dissipates as we grow up because life itself has shown us the harsh reality. What a shame, right? How beautiful our heart was all those years ago ... Why did it have to be darkened?

But don't worry, there is good news. We are going to bring back the light and beauty your heart deserves, and you will realise that the love you once felt as a child is still there. That wasn't an illusion – that was really you. That precious little girl full of love and joy for life was your true self and you are still her, because you're still here ... you. You just have to awaken.

Reflection: Meet your child self

Find a photo of yourself from when you were a child. Or maybe you already have one in your head that you remember. I want you to observe that little girl's eyes. What do you see? What do you perceive in the depths of them? Tenderness, softness, innocence, love, joy? Maybe some sadness already? What we all find in that child's eyes is purity; she is pure and open to receiving whatever the world and the adults around her give her.

Look at her face and try to realise that whatever is within her is still within you right now. That same innocence and purity is in you. It's only that you've covered it with everything you've learnt and all the protections you've had to build around yourself. Try for a second to get inside her mind and look at your current surroundings through her eyes, and feel that amazement for life.

It's almost inevitable that you will smile while you're doing this, because at that point in your life you were so excited to be here, you were so loving, everything seemed so magical ... everything around you was a reflection of your love.

You know you can go back to looking at life in that way, right? If only you weren't ashamed of being so innocent, or fearful of being exposed when you're so loving or criticised for being such a joyful dreamer. I wish we didn't have to pretend we were so mature, strong, effective, so put together ... and we dared to just be that little girl again, and have fun, and enjoy our lives with calm and purity.

The more you practise this reflective exercise, the more you will feel familiar with that sense of authenticity that we all so desperately need. And you know what? You might just find that you can be an inspiration for others, too.

CHAPTER 5
Our Script, Our Values

'First say to yourself what you would be; and then do what you have to do.'

– Epictetus

When I ask the question, 'Who are you?' people tend to respond by describing their profession, their current life situation and their gender or sexual identity. 'I'm a doctor, I'm a mum, I'm a woman.' Then I go deeper: 'But *who* are you?' And now they describe themselves. 'I'm a person who loves dogs and sports, I'm a workaholic, I'm an extrovert, and sociable.' Or they tell me about their past, saying how this and that happened to them, so they are now this way. All these answers are based on external factors in the outside world. Either they are comparing themselves to others so then decide what they are like after measuring themselves against that scale, or they see how they feel about certain experiences and then label themselves accordingly.

We all do this. We create a self from what we experience. And this self is added to the self we have developed so far in life through the influences of our culture, education and religion. It is through this constructed self that we act, live and love.

We come up with a character for the script we have written of our life; we tell ourselves that this is who we are, and present ourselves to others this way. We feel safe doing this because we can know ourselves this way. We know how we need to react, how to talk, how to move – our character is familiar to us, to the point where we don't even mind being enslaved by the description we have written. And if, in any given situation, we are instinctively going to react in a different way, we immediately revert to how we must react in order to comply with being the person we believe we are.

I would like us to shift this perspective; why don't we find out who we truly are?

When we are kids, we just are ourselves, in essence. We laugh all the time; we create; we move; we observe; we're curious; we're intrigued by how things work; or we're just floating on a cloud. But then we grow up, often in a family that has certain values, and gradually we learn those values. We go to school and they teach us other values, some of them perhaps aligned with our family's, and we make friends who have other values, some of them aligned with ours but others aligned with their own family's. We live in a neighbourhood, a city, a country, a continent, where the society around has its own values, which we learn and respect and integrate into our personality as our own. We might have a religious faith, too, which teaches us other values still, and we absorb these as well. So we end up full of values and morals that we decide are going to be our guides for living, interacting and growing as a person.

This might all seem fine, but then why do we end up having so many misunderstandings, so many fights, so many arguments with those around us who supposedly share our values? Well, perhaps because not everyone has grown in the same way as we have, or experienced what we have. Everyone has their own particular script dictating who they are and how they should behave in different situations.

Again, there is nothing right or wrong about this; inevitably, we all judge people and situations depending on our script and our values. And yes, we definitely need to know who we are and what we believe in, in order to decide how to live. But what happens when we feel discomfort with the way we live? What happens when we start questioning what we have been taught? Well, that's when the magic happens. Then we can open our minds and realise that maybe the person we think we are is not who we truly are.

Different species

Imagine you live in a jungle. There are all sorts of animals living in there. Snakes, monkeys, tigers, birds ... But in this jungle, when a baby is born, they are not necessarily the same species as their parents.

Let's say both parents are tigers, but their child is born a monkey. The two tigers, however, assume that their child is also a tiger, so they will teach them all about how to be a tiger – what to eat, how to move, how to hunt. They will teach them the dangers of the jungle, the poisonous fruits, the water to drink from the good river, and so on, always from a tiger's point of view. That baby monkey, when it's first born, will behave like a monkey, a little lazy maybe, wanting to hug trees instead of hunting, all smiley and tender ... but as they are being raised as a tiger, inevitably they will grow up as if they were a tiger, with the same thinking patterns and values, the script very well memorised about who they are and who they need to be.

This child grows up hiding its monkey truth, perhaps not even paying attention to it, not daring to find within itself values that don't match with the tiger they think they are.

Inevitably, this monkey will look for friends that are tiger-like, for a partner that is a tiger (or maybe a panther or a puma), and often they will find those who think they are tigers, too, though that might also be a facade, so they will relate to each other on that false level. As a result, this monkey will feel lonely when it sits in silence with itself, it will feel misunderstood, and it won't know how to erase that sadness or unease with life. So, it will find ways to numb that feeling, with pleasures or disconnection, because it doesn't want to feel that hole inside.

Of course, you're probably thinking, *This animal needs to realise it's a monkey, not a tiger,* but the only way to get to that truth is by daring to go there. If it does, maybe the monkey will discover pure tenderness, the joy of living, authenticity. Maybe it won't care any more about the core tiger values of hunting or fighting, but about other values that are more aligned with who it truly is.

This is what can happen to us if we construct a set of values for ourselves that mask who we really are. We might not be the same species as our parents. Sometimes our parents might not even be the same species as each other, even though they have things in common, so the messages we get from them can be confusing. You might relate more to one than the other, or maybe one of them has compromised their true essence in order to fit in with their own family, friends or partner, and so has modelled that behaviour to you. Eventually your parents might get divorced, and you are left with two different concepts of life, neither of which is your own. Maybe they, too, weren't really who they showed themselves to be.

The lesson is, we need to realise what we dream of, what makes us happy and what makes us feel in sync with the flow of life. If we discover what brings us joy, what our talents and passions are, we can learn who we are meant to be and what we are meant to do in this life – not necessarily through our learnt values, but through our love for who we really are, admiration for all we can do, and respect and understanding that this jungle needs all sorts of animals to function as it should.

Working together

When thinking about our values, it is vital for us to realise that we are all working together to make our communities work. We are all different, all unique and important, and we're all bringing something valuable to the table. But first, we need to realise what kind of animal we are to be true to our potential and capacities. And if we realise we are a monkey, not a tiger, then we can decide where we want to be, how we want to live and what we can contribute to our relationships and our society. We must respect and embrace other ways of living and acting, and understand that we are in this together.

To do this, we all need values, as individuals and as a society. And ideally these values come from love, not from a learnt script. You can be taught certain values from when you are a kid, but if they don't come from your heart, eventually you will rebel against them. If your values are grounded in love, however, they will come naturally and won't need to be taught. Kindness, respect, honesty, compassion, humility ... these values are necessary if we are to form meaningful, fulfilling relationships with others, but they need to be in your heart, as that's the only way you will apply them to yourself and others. And if you encounter someone who doesn't share them for some reason, then, with compassion, you will step away from them.

Then there are the values we learn in order to thrive in our environment; these are agreed on between the group or community. But as they are learnt values, they can fall dangerously into grey areas. Big values like not harming others can become misunderstood when we're talking about defending ourselves or our people, as can honesty when it comes to protecting someone you care for. Judging in these instances can be tricky, because we don't necessarily share the same values as others or would have done things differently. Other people might defend what they did from their point of view, and it can be very hard to convince them they are wrong, as their story might be totally different to ours.

Again, only by being true to our human values, which are true love and true compassion – for your loved ones and for your enemies – and by recognising that we are all in this together and need each other for everything to function, will we be able to respect each other. Don't you think this is the best way to start rewriting the harming dynamics we may be locked into?

This applies to ourselves first and foremost, as we need to understand our own values and to love who we are before we can live the way we deserve and bring benefits to the communities we are part of. It's vital to break down that wall that protects our heart and explore our core values, as it's the only way to create authentic change in us and in others.

Reflection: Get to know your values

I'm going to ask you now to try to connect with your true values. 'But how?' you might ask. Well, the same way you have connected to them at certain moments in the past.

For example, when the Twin Towers catastrophe happened in New York on 11 September 2001, we all remember where we were when we watched that unfolding. Practically the whole globe

Our Script, Our Values

was watching by the time the second plane hit the tower. We were all in shock, crying, feeling as if it was happening to us. Most of us didn't know any of the victims who were there suffering. We might never even have been to New York or have known the towers existed, but we were suffering as if those people were our brothers and sisters. We were feeling one with each other. It was horrible and indescribably sad, but the amount of love we all felt for people we didn't know, the compassion that filled our hearts, those are our true values. We didn't ask their names, or their race, their gender, their sexual orientation or their social class ... we just loved them.

It also happened, for example, during the devastating tsunami in Indonesia in 2004. So many people from all over the world were feeling pain at what happened, even though it wasn't happening to them. Many people, from all over the world, sent all kinds of items and food, others even travelled there to help. Many followed the news every single day, trying to find out whether there were more survivors, as if members of their own families were there.

Do you realise that is who we are? Inside, we know we are one and that whatever happens to one person is happening to all the others.

Observe your own instinct when someone falls next to you, or when a child is crying, lost, in the middle of a crowd, or when someone is attacked or in pain near you ... You immediately feel it in your heart, but then your rational mind might kick in and start thinking, *No, getting involved can be dangerous*, or, *No, I might get in trouble if I help*, or, *No, I'm going to be late* ... Next time, connect to that instinct, and know that every single person on this planet has that instinct, too.

So, what I ask of you in this reflection is to observe your reactions. Are they coming from the heart? From your thinking mind? Are they based on fear and caution, or love and compassion? Think about it and get to know yourself.

CHAPTER 6
The Game of Life

'The first and best victory is conquering yourself.'
– Plato

From a spiritual perspective, some say that before coming into this life, we choose what we will live through in order to achieve our goal, which is to find ourselves and realise who we are and what we are made of. We choose beforehand to receive signs that gradually open our eyes, and it is up to us, and how we use our free will, whether we become aware of them or refuse to see the path that will truly lead us to our goal.

The main goal of the soul is to experience all sort of emotions so it can eventually find and experience their true essence, which is love. In other words, left would never know that it is left until it sees and reflects the right. Light would never know that it is light until it experiences darkness.

This is the only purpose in life, the only mission – to find ourselves, know ourselves, experience ourselves and enjoy ourselves. But until we reach that point, we will generally meet people or find ourselves in situations that will make us feel the same 'bad' or uncomfortable things over and over again. We all have free will to make decisions and choose different paths, and the ability to decide not to do what our intuition is guiding us to do, but the goal of finding ourselves remains the same. It depends on you whether you choose to darken the experience of reaching that goal by relying too much on the workings of the human mind, or whether you open up to the wisdom inside you and let that guide you. Like the river that will end up in the sea, we flow towards our destiny. We will inevitably meet obstacles, but that free will we all have can be used either to let go of control and enjoy the flow, learning from the challenges along the way, or to perpetually take some other route, thinking we will avoid the obstacles, or that we know better.

You may not yet believe that there is a spiritual meaning to our history. If that is the case, may I just ask you to open your mind and your heart and be willing to see some of the signs if they are given to you? Intuition, sensations, coincidences ... they all have something to teach us.

Life is amazing – truly amazing. If you look at it from a certain perspective, you realise how magical and perfectly wonderful it is. The spiritual teacher Eckhart Tolle says, 'Suffering is necessary until you realise that it is not necessary to suffer.' We have to go through things that will make us suffer so that we can discover our strength, our tastes, our essence; in short, so that we can discover who we are. And the sooner we discover it, the sooner we will truly enjoy life.

If you looked back and thought about all the 'bad' things that have happened to you, and then I asked you, 'What have you learnt from those experiences?' could you answer me? Do you think that negative experiences have gifted you any life lessons? If so, perfect! That is the intention. If not, get ready, because life has a habit of teaching you that same lesson over and over again, more strongly each time, until you are able to open your eyes and truly learn it. It's as if you experience a reality that matches the level of understanding you have, and you will only get to the next level when you have seen the clues, taken them onboard and opened the door to the next level. In effect, you will upgrade your level of understanding through the discomfort you will feel with the experiences you have.

There are people who say, 'I don't believe in those things. There are no lessons. Things happen to you because they happen, and that's it. Some people are more prone to certain experiences and others maybe just have better luck.' I greatly respect that statement, but what happens when you look more closely at what has happened to you? What if I told you that you will find a common thread in everything that has been happening to you? I would love to be with you right now as you recall the memories of your life's trajectory. Take a moment and think about all the people who have hurt you, for example, because if you do so, you will realise that they have made you experience the same feeling, over and over again. And when you realise that they always touch the same key, you have no choice but to pay attention, look inwards and try to resolve the root cause of that uncomfortable emotion so that it can finally disappear, and that will be a lesson learnt.

Almost all of us, to a greater or lesser extent, experience feelings that, at their core, are similar. We feel like we are not understood, we are abandoned, we are hurt, we are not heard, we are disappointed. And all of these feelings have almost nothing to do with the person who causes them; they have to do with us and our inner selves. We should use this knowledge to find the key to life, which is to find ourselves, truly. Ask yourself: *Where am I within all that is happening to me?*

Thanks to everything we have experienced in life, most of us will be able to find ourselves sooner or later... and it's wonderful. The sad thing is, if we don't realise this, we are always going to live life feeling like a victim of someone or something. But the truth is that we are only ever victims of ourselves, because we, too, repeatedly look for the people and situations that will make us feel the same as we have before.

This happens because it is human nature to always seek out those familiar emotions that feel comfortable to us and through which we can be ourselves, according to the identity we have constructed. It also happens because we somehow know that we have to heal our wounds, and, as we discussed in Chapter 4, in order to locate them in the first place we need others to touch them so that they hurt us. Once our wounds are healed, we no longer need the kind of people who will hurt us, so we stop getting sucked into the same dynamic again and again. It's that simple, and that complicated. And when all of this happens at a subconscious level, which you are not aware of because you're too busy living, well, then that state is even harder for you to reach. But don't worry, you will get there, and the effort will be worth it.

So, it's important that today you are willing to look at yourself and see your wounds, without judging them, without judging yourself and without judging the one who caused them or reminded you that they were there. Just try to see your wounds; look at them and acknowledge them. It's okay, I dare you to do it ... Do you feel like a little abandoned child? Do you think you've done things wrong and feel guilty? Are you afraid to face life alone because you see yourself as fragile? Do you feel guilty because you believe that you haven't done something well or could have done it better? Or maybe you don't feel worthy of true love or good enough for anyone?

Whatever you feel, it's okay, it's perfect; that's just what you need to feel, exactly that, even if it hurts, even if it embarrasses you, even if you're afraid. Feel it. It's necessary to expose yourself to that pain in order to realise many things. Every emotion has something to teach us.

Playing the game

Let's remember, life presents us with situations or people to make us feel certain things, so that we then learn something about ourselves. If we do not learn the lesson, or do not learn it deeply enough, the same thing, in a different way, will be presented to us again until we overcome that obstacle and move on to the next one.

I like to use the metaphor of a videogame where at the end of each level there is a monster to kill. Throughout that particular level, you have been jumping over obstacles that gain you extra weapons, or you have been accumulating powers that sufficiently prepare you to face the final monster. The first few times you play, you fall into some of the traps, but as you play again and again, you progress more easily, and there comes a time when you know perfectly where the weapons are hidden and what things give you strength, and so you begin to reach the final monster much more easily. Each time you face the monster, you learn better how to kill it, but the first few times you try it kills you, and you have to start the game over again – sometimes not right back from the beginning, but from a certain point, which then becomes the starting point next time the damn monster kills you. And so you try again and again, hooked on the game, learning where to shoot, and at what moment ... until one day, you manage to finish it! And what presents itself to you? The next level, of course. And in this next level there are even trickier obstacles than in the previous one, and it takes several games to learn how to advance, and well, when you get to the monster on this level, you have to learn how to kill that one, because it is even more difficult to vanquish than the previous one.

You know where I'm going with this, right? The game, of course, is our life: the first few levels are easier, but complicated for a beginner, so you have to learn level by level, monster by monster, and until you learn how to navigate the obstacles, you cannot move forward.

You are going to keep having the same types of relationships that cause you pain because you are, in effect, stuck on the same level of your videogame, going through it again and again. Despite the negative experiences you are suffering, you are not taking on board the lessons, and you are going to keep reacting in the same way until you realise that you're not going about it in the right way, that you have to turn in another direction. You are only stuck there to pick up a weapon, a tool, a skill, but you haven't managed to slay the monster yet, even though this level has been preparing you for it.

There are lives and lives, paths and paths; each one of us has our own path – we can give each other advice, set examples for one another, but each one of us has our own game to play. Each of us chooses which one it will be. Even when we know that we will be 'killed' over and over again, we still have fun trying. Why? Because the feeling of having overcome a level after trying so hard is irreplaceable! Perhaps the difference is that here, in our reality, we only have one life. (Unless, of course, you believe in reincarnation ...) So, during the game of life, our only chance is running out – but our life can also be recharged. Every time we find love or joy, whenever we are living in the moment, absorbed and fulfilled, our energy for life recharges.

It's like finding a booster that refills the cup of life. Scientists are now investigating our life span and how to expand it ... well, I think the answer could be quite simple: life is equal to love (within ourselves, for others and for life). The more we love, the more life, health and energy we have. And remember, you will not recharge your life by only loving others and neglecting yourself; inevitably yours will run out.

In the end, it's just a matter of taking it all as a wonderful and incredibly intense adventure. Remember, whatever we do, sooner or later it will be 'Game Over', and then it will all just end. The game deserves to be fully enjoyed – it's such a wonderful gift.

Fear

Teresa was a beautiful, smart, cheerful girl who grew up very happy until her mother died of an incurable disease when Teresa was just 15. Her father, who could not bear the pain, left, abandoning his daughter in her hometown. She was alone, with no siblings, no aunts or uncles. Thanks to some acquaintances, she was able to finish school, and at the age of 18 she moved to the big city to try to build a life for herself. She suffered greatly from the loss of her mother and the abandonment of her father, and the resulting loneliness, but she was a strong girl with very clear ideas, and she decided to move forward. In the city, she looked for work as a waitress, rented a room in a shared apartment and began to live her life. On the surface, everything was fine, despite the drama she had experienced. She only had one problem – she argued a lot with her boyfriend, whom she met while working as a waitress. He was a very nice guy, and they hit it off right away. Teresa mostly got along very well with him and his family,

The Game of Life

who in her lonely state became like family to her. She never argued with anyone apart from her boyfriend – and their conflicts were fierce. She would scream, cry, sometimes almost hit him in a hurricane of emotion that he, somehow, went along with. And so the relationship continued. Some days were great, others were terrible. They both knew they couldn't go on like this; it was unbearable. Moreover, to avoid arguing, they lied or hid things from each other, which ended up causing even greater storms, but neither dared to end the relationship, because they loved each other.

I've only summarised Teresa's story in brief, but what do you think? We may have different opinions, but we all surely agree on one thing: this is not a healthy relationship, even if there is love at its core.

So, what happened? Teresa and her boyfriend ended the relationship after a couple of years, realising how toxic it was. They remained friends, and Teresa still almost felt like part of his family, but they were no longer a couple.

All went well until Teresa met another guy. At first, it was a delight. He was wonderful, and she was happy. *Oh, this is a beautiful relationship*, she thought. *I feel so good. This could be the one.* Do you know how long this idyllic phase lasted? I'll tell you: a month at most. What happened? The first argument came. He went out with his friends, told her he would be home soon and would call her when he got there, but he actually got home at seven in the morning and then called her the next day instead. Teresa was angry and hurt. 'Why didn't you call me when you got home?' she demanded.

'Because it was too late – I wasn't going to call you at that time.'

'Why didn't you let me know?' she asked.

'Because I got distracted.'

It Starts With You

Teresa didn't want to overreact, so she let it go and they made plans to meet at his house in the afternoon. At first everything was fine, but there came a point where she couldn't hold it in any more and said, 'Was it too hard for you to send me a message to let me know you weren't going to call me? I was waiting, and if I had known, I would have gone to sleep instead of looking like a fool waiting for your call.'

'I'm sorry,' he said. 'I really didn't realise you were waiting.'

What type of response do you think she gave?

- **A.** 'Okay, no problem, but please let me know next time. How was your day?'
- **B.** 'How could you not realise it? Do you forget about me that quickly? What's going on? Were there other girls with you and that's why you didn't think to message me?'

That's right, she went with option B ... and so it continued, with accusations, doubts, shouting, tears and slamming doors. Exactly the same as what happened with her previous boyfriend, but with one aggravating factor: this guy had also gone through some tough times and would get just as upset as her, or more. And so the arguments between these two escalated even higher, even stronger, both of them crying, both of them becoming furious – and it went on like that for four years. The pattern of Teresa being taken in by his family, who adored her, was repeated, but the relationship was completely unbearable, and yet they continued.

Today, Teresa is single, but do you think it will go well for her when she finds a new partner? Do you think things can be healed by leaving a relationship, being alone for a while, and then starting another?

The Game of Life

No, because that's not how you heal. It's not a matter of swapping the current partner for a better boyfriend who won't hurt you, or even realising that you need to improve your way of reacting. It goes deeper than that. Because – as we can all understand – she was 'abandoned' by her mother and father, so as soon as she perceives a hint of possible abandonment from her partner, she can't bear it. She doesn't know how to handle it. The fear of being abandoned again by someone she loves consumes her.

What Teresa has experienced is very common. When your partner doesn't listen to you or understand you, you feel alone. When your coworkers misjudge you, you feel misunderstood. When your mother supports your siblings more than you and justifies what they've done, you feel inadequate. When your partner chooses to spend their free time with other people or doing activities without you, you feel rejected. When you come home alone and feel like everyone else has their life together but you can't fill yours, you feel shame. In all those moments when you feel judged, misunderstood, alone and empty, what are you really feeling? What's behind that pressure in your chest, that knot in your stomach, that pang in your throat?

Behind all that, there's only one thing.

FEAR.

Fear of being alone and suffering; fear of not being loved and suffering; fear of being abandoned by him or her and suffering; fear of not being good enough; fear of . . . it happening to me again . . . yes, it happening to me AGAIN.

Unfortunately, when you were that little ball of love as a little girl, something happened that made you feel afraid. Whether it was confusion, mistrust or betrayal, it made you feel afraid, and, since then, that fear has stayed with you because that's when you discovered it, and every time you've faced something that reminds you of what you felt then, it only makes the fear greater. And you know what? You're going to experience a lot of things that are going to touch that wound. When your boyfriend doesn't call you, you'll feel helpless; when your children don't appreciate you, you'll feel small and insecure; when your friends do certain things, you'll feel jealous or inferior. Why? Because of fear.

So then, what is healing all about? Well, it's solely about *you*. It's about getting to know yourself, facing your fears, loving yourself and being with yourself.

What do we want?

What are we really looking for in life? To be happy? To have the best time possible? Can you even answer this? I talked to a friend recently who told me that she has been feeling depressed lately. She stopped working years ago to take care of her children. Her husband is very successful at his job and is very generous with all the money he makes, since he values the tremendous work she puts into taking care of the house and family. But she's down. She finds it difficult to wake up happy in the mornings. She can't blame anyone because her children are lovely and her husband is amazing, but she's not happy. I listen to her as we have a cup of green tea, and when she finishes telling me about her distress, I ask her a simple question, 'What would make you happy?'

After an eternal silence, she replies, 'Oh, I don't know. I really have everything. I don't know what's wrong with me. I don't know what I'm complaining about.' If she thinks that her husband should work less and be at home with her more, she realises she doesn't want that because they would have less money, and her husband is passionate about his work, so it would be unfair to him. If she thinks about spending less time with her children so that she can focus more on herself, she realises she doesn't want that either, because she loves spending time with her children, and it wouldn't be worth doing things that make her happy but that take her away from her children. In reality, being a mother is what fills her up the most in the world right now. So then, why isn't she happy? What would she answer if a genie in a bottle materialised in front of her and offered her the chance to live her ideal life?

The truth is that for many of us it's totally impossible to answer this question, because we don't know what would make us happy. We don't even know what happiness is. We might assume we want such and such a thing, and if we don't have that yet it might seem easier to answer the question, as we can find a specific reason for our unhappiness, but if we happen to have all that supposedly makes us happy, why aren't we? Why do we keep searching for more? Well, it's not possible to imagine happiness with our minds, it's not possible to be happy if we only think logically. If all your energy is tied up in your thoughts, in your ambitions, in your expectations, they will never get fulfilled.

It can be challenging to try to visualise our ideal life. Even scary! Thoughts like *I don't deserve it, This is impossible, Would this be the right choice? This would be unfair to such and such a person, This can't happen to me* can sneak in. In other words, we start sabotaging our own lives by the simple act of imagining it. But why? Well, generally, it's due to a lack of habit. Almost every time we think of an imaginary future, our head imagines the worst possible scenario. It imagines all the bad things that could happen as a way to prepare us for suffering, so that we can cope with it. As a result, we're not used to thinking of an ideal situation full of happiness, with all the luxury of details. We're not used to really thinking about what we want; we haven't been taught how to do it, and we don't see the people around us doing it either, so it even seems a bit selfish. Not to mention that it can also seem stupid – surely, we can't be so naive as to think that we can attain a perfect life? But it's also difficult for us to imagine it because of fear. Why fear? Because if I dare to imagine that perfect life, day by day, then what? I open my eyes and I am faced with my reality, and I get depressed, so it's better not to try.

So, what do we want? How can we expect someone or something to make us happy if we don't even let ourselves imagine being happy?

The goal is to appreciate the opportunity of playing this game of life, and to be happy because we still have a life to go through, with its challenges as well as the beautiful experiences, and to enjoy it all fully ... and to get to 'Game Over' feeling proud of the way we played.

Reflection: Your ideal life

Let's try another reflection. What do you want? What would make you exultantly happy? If a genie materialised in front of you, looked into your eyes with great love and said, 'What is your ideal life? How do you want your days to be? What do you want your future to look like? Tell me, and I will make it happen for you,' would you be able to answer? Would you be able to say what you want in detail?

If you don't know, take a moment and think about it. Close your eyes and visualise this entity in front of you offering you the ideal life you desire, but only if you can describe it. Think about your perfect life, with as many details as you can.

Try to visualise your perfect day from the moment you wake up: where are you? And with whom? What is your house like? What are you planning for today? Or are you going to sleep in and stay at home? Are you moving fast and energetically, or are you feeling slow and reflective? What is the weather like? Are you in a beach house, a mountain cottage, a city apartment or a town house? Do you have all your family at home or is it just you? What is your ideal? Maybe your ideal is to wake up each day in a different place and be a different person? Why not? One day you are a single, successful lawyer, the next day you are a housewife with five children, preparing breakfast for everyone. You can imagine anything you want, and this all-powerful entity will make it come true, but remember, only if you give them all the details.

It Starts With You

The important thing to realise here is that I've simply asked you to spend a few minutes of your time imagining supreme happiness with all the luxury of details, and it's very likely that you won't be able to, or that you'll at least find it very difficult. I'm not even saying that you should try to enact it, or that you should leave your life and go in search of true happiness. Nor am I encouraging you to do anything by telling you that everything is possible. I'm just asking you to imagine it, and yet for most people it's so much harder than you might imagine.

Don't worry – this is all part of the process. Realising this is a major step towards finding true happiness, because we learn that we might be blindly or automatically looking for happiness, without knowing what that really means for us or where to find it. We just need to learn that happiness is a way of living, and that the source of it lies within us.

CHAPTER 7
The Cycle of Longing

'It is hard to free fools from the chains they worship.'
— Voltaire

Society paints happiness as a state you reach when everything is going well. When you have love, money, time, health and beauty. *Of course,* you think, *having all of that means being happy! Well then, as soon as I have all that, I'll be super-happy, right?* But have you noticed that no matter what we have in our life, it never seems to be enough? True happiness still seems to elude us, and we end up in a cycle of perpetual longing for something different, regardless of our circumstances.

Our thought loops might look something like this: *I'm looking for a partner who fulfils me, takes care of me, protects me. Someone who is fun, who listens to me, understands me, respects me and gives me freedom, who is affectionate and also feels fulfilled. If I don't have love, I won't be happy.* But as soon as we notice that our partner is lacking in any of the points that we believe they should have in order for the love bucket to be filled to the brim, we get scared. We think: *Oh God, this isn't right, you're not supposed to love me like this.*

Maybe we don't have our parents any more, and if that's the case, well, it's almost impossible to overcome the sadness of losing them. We might feel empty, without roots, without emotional sustenance. But if we do have them, we complain about them. 'But, Mum, it's not supposed to be like this.' 'Oh, Dad, can you just let me do what I want?' In the end, we don't feel 100 per cent loved by them either, and perhaps even when we look at them, we blame them in some way for the childhood we had and what we have become.

If we don't have money, we might think: *I can't afford anything. How am I going to pay my bills?* And yet, when we have a little money, we think, *Oh, I can't spend too much, I have to be smart. I can't just waste money on things I want, no matter how much I like them. If I had more, everything would be easier and I would be so happy, able to buy anything without worrying about the price. I know money doesn't bring happiness, but if only I had a bit more money, I could do everything I want and how I want.*

And even when we have a lot of money, we might think, *People only like me for my money – of course – since they know I pay when we go out. They don't realise that I have problems. People envy me; I can't show off everything I have because it makes them feel bad. And the conversations I have with other wealthy people are so superficial ... If I had less money, maybe my life would be more authentic?*

And then there's the question of time. Between work, studies, children, going here and there, we often feel like we don't have time for anything. *I don't have time for myself. I don't have time to talk to my friends, to call my parents, to enjoy nature, to dedicate myself to my hobbies. Oh, if only I had time to do what I really want, I would be so happy. If I had free time, I would be with my people, I would really enjoy life.*

Or, if we feel like we have too much free time, we might tell ourselves, *The world falls on me. I don't know what to do with my life. I don't know what to do with my time.*

Many of us worry about staying healthy, thinking, *I need to eat well, but I love pizza, bread, hamburgers. I need to exercise, but I don't have time and I don't feel like it – I don't have enough motivation, so it's hard for me to get started. Organic food is very expensive, and healthy food doesn't have any taste.* And even if we are really healthy, we can end up feeling like we're not doing enough: *I eat well, I don't smoke, I don't drink, but still I'm not 100 per cent, so I guess I just need to keep trying. Or maybe I need to take supplements or do intermittent fasting. I'm going to go online and see what the latest health trends are.*

If we have some kind of disease or live with some physical pain, we tell ourselves, *If only I were totally healthy, I would be so happy. If nothing hurt, if I got to rest well, all my problems would be solved.*

And all too many of us fixate on how we look and compare ourselves to others. Maybe we think, *I'm too fat*, or, *I'm too skinny*, or, *Oh, I'm getting wrinkles, and my hair is going grey. Look at those people on TV and social media. I'm sure they've had surgery, but I don't have the money for that. If only I were tall, skinny, young and beautiful, I would be so happy. Being beautiful opens so many doors for you – I would find a good partner, and a better job.*

Even if we are blessed with great beauty, we still face challenges: *I'm judged on my looks – no one takes me seriously. I always have to prove that I'm intelligent. If I weren't so beautiful, everything would be easier.*

We can go round in circles forever picking holes in how we look, what we have and who we are. We spend our days explaining to ourselves why we are not completely happy and blaming our shortcomings for it. And we kill ourselves trying to achieve what we believe will make us happy, or beat ourselves up, feeling that we will never have or be enough to achieve it. Incessantly besieged by our thoughts, we miss the truth about the real source of happiness – that which gives us a perfect and crystal-clear lens through which to look at life and at ourselves. Even if you have all the love from others, all the money, time, good health and beauty in the world, if you don't have that essential love, that all-important connection to your true self, no, my friend, you won't be fundamentally happy. That's the first thing you need. That is the thing that will make you feel calm, satisfied, powerful, confident and connected to everyone... basically, HAPPY.

In fact, it's the other way around! If you're happy, you'll probably find that you won't feel as if you need any of that external stuff.

Filling the void

There is something that almost all human beings have in common, at least in our Western society. A kind of internal emptiness that accompanies us wherever we go, which nothing and no one can really fill. Sometimes we realise it, sometimes we don't. Sometimes we hide it by taking substances or keeping ourselves busy, but when we are alone and have nothing to do, there it is, that emptiness – our inseparable companion. With smart phones it is now easier to ignore it because as soon as we have a moment when we have nothing to do, we jump to the screen and gorge ourselves on whatever is on it – entertainment, classes, friends, videos, celebrities. Very rarely do we decide to face the silence.

You can be a superwoman with a great job, or have children or grandchildren who fill your soul, or a partner whom you love very much, or wonderful friends, but when you are alone with nothing to focus on, you can still have that internal feeling. And, of course, if you don't face it, if you live but not

The Cycle of Longing

from within, if you don't dare to stop and look inside to find out what that feeling is and what it is you are missing so deeply, it will never go away. Yes, perhaps you can go through life without paying attention to it, but that emptiness will give you the impulse to fill it with things or people, and it will bring you problems and conflicts in your relationships with people, with work, with the world in general and with yourself.

The truth is that we are always accompanied by any conscious or unconscious traumatic memory that we have suffered in our childhood, and this produces loneliness, sadness and that feeling of emptiness. So, how can we tackle this? How can we have healthy relationships? How can we be happy if we are carrying around all this longing that we sometimes don't even know is there, that we don't want to see or have no idea how to resolve?

What if, once and for all, we decided to face that emptiness and longing, to find out what it is and where it comes from, to truly and forever fill the void we feel inside? What if we set out to achieve inner peace and harmony so we can live life in absolute fullness, in love, in gratitude, so that no matter what happens on the outside, our inner selves are so immense and firm that nothing can even come close to throwing us off balance? Do you know how your life and the lives of the people around you would change? You would truly be contributing, not just a bit, but a huge amount, to the solution to the world's greatest problem: a lack of love.

There are no tricks, no more turns to take. The only thing that will solve all our problems is love – the essence, the nature, of what you're made of. You might say, 'Ha-ha, it's very simple, I just need to love everyone and then all my problems will disappear.' Or you might think, *Yes, this all sounds very beautiful and mystical, but I have real problems ... and besides, I don't even know what love she's talking about.*

It Starts With You

Before you overthink it, listen to me and open your heart. Take a long, deep, slow breath and give me a chance to explain it to you.

When you can feel this love that I'm talking about, you'll stop being afraid. You won't fear anything or anyone. You'll feel peace and calm. You won't expect anything from anyone or anything. You won't demand that anyone do anything, you'll simply be able to live, have peace and feel fulfilled. And then you won't need anything to make you happy because you already would be, and everything you have will be a wonderful addition to your life, which you'll experience with joy, peace and harmony.

And if something happens to you that hurts, you'll feel it, you'll cry, you'll look at it, accept it, and then calmly, little by little, you'll learn to integrate it however you need to. As a lesson, as a tool or just as acceptance. Without fear, without anxiety, without guilt, but with acceptance, without running away from the pain, because although it will hurt, it won't make you suffer.

You'll stop constantly worrying, you'll stop always looking for problems to solve, you'll allow yourself to relax and let the Earth keep spinning without feeling like you have to control anything for that to happen. You'll let the river flow naturally without trying to stop it. You'll dance simply to enjoy the movement. Wherever you go, whether on easier or harder paths, fast or calm waters, you'll make your way feeling relaxed, observing your surroundings, not on alert, but in peace. You'll enjoy your journey and your life. You'll love yourself ... and you'll be loved.

Yes, it sounds utopian, but I assure you it's real. I assure you that you can have exactly the same life you have right now, but if you can feel what I'm saying, it will seem like a totally different and wonderful life to you. And if you don't find it wonderful, then you'll feel capable of taking the risks needed to change it, because you won't be afraid. You'll love life in all its glory. Because you'll know there's a safety net that supports you, there to catch you in case you fall. Now, you'll be ready to live.

Reflection: Identify your longing

What are you looking for that you think will bring you happiness when you get it? Is it money, beauty, love from others? Which desire is the one that sucks most of your energy? What do you work towards? Try to define it. What do you envy in others?

Once you've identified it, think about why you feel you need it. Besides 'to be happy', what do you need it for specifically? Because as long as you have the basics, you're good. Yes, you could always have more and be better, but if you don't accept your current situation, whatever that is, you won't be able to start working towards what you want from the right place. You will always want more, you will always want to be better.

You need more money? What for? So you can buy more stuff to feel happier? And if that doesn't work, you'll feel compelled to try to make more money and buy even more stuff? You need more beauty? What is beauty anyway? Are you going to try to meet those standards we are bombarded with just to make us feel more insecure?

It Starts With You

Maybe you long for better health? Well, this is a big one, yes ... Certainly, the healthier we are, the better we feel. But is your lack of health a product of your lack of self-love? Are you poisoning yourself with bad habits, harmful chemicals such as drugs and alcohol, or even the stress chemicals that negative thinking triggers in us? More self-love, better connections and greater acceptance would definitely improve your health, so you can then start dealing with the struggle you haven't been able to control, from a much stronger place.

I want you to think about all of this as part of this reflection. I can't give you all the answers – I wouldn't even try to. I understand that each individual is in their own unique situation. I'm just here to try to help you ask the questions, to maybe open a new path, a new dynamic for your thoughts, which might take you to a better place.

CHAPTER 8
Good or Bad?

'I know that I know nothing.'
– Socrates

After a relationship breakdown, my friend Elena moved back in with her mum and dad, who were not very old. They lived a comfortable life together, and all loved each other very much, but this did not prevent Elena and her parents from having great arguments that left Elena feeling disoriented, frustrated and tremendously vulnerable. One of the most frequently recurring fights was about health. Elena was a vegan, who always ate organic, gluten-free and lactose-free food when possible. She was very much involved in the world of meditation, and physical, mental and spiritual health. Her parents, on the other hand, were not at all like this. They ate unhealthy food, occasionally drank alcohol, smoked and, although they had a happy life, didn't take much extra care. They didn't really believe in 'modern lifestyle trends' as they called them.

Elena was okay with it as long as she didn't have to live it up close. She had lived in Paris for many years, where she had got engaged to a guy with whom she had a son. When the relationship didn't work out, she moved back to Madrid to live with her parents, who welcomed her with open arms and were delighted to take care of their precious grandson. They took him to school and to birthday parties, while Elena worked, so they were a great help to her.

At first, Elena didn't say anything every time her parents ate tinned food or ready-meals, or ordered fast food. She didn't like it, but she only commented on it occasionally. After a while, however, her mother had a serious health problem, which meant she had to be admitted to the hospital for a few weeks before returning home. This health incident didn't make her parents improve their way of living; instead, it worsened, because her mother had mobility problems and got tired from cooking or going for walks. Elena had a tough time while her mother was in the hospital, and the first big fight came shortly after she was discharged.

One day, Elena woke up and found her parents having breakfast from a fast food restaurant. 'What are you doing?' she asked them.

'Your father went out to buy the newspaper and brought breakfast back,' her mother replied. 'Besides, there was an offer of two complete breakfasts with eggs and bacon for the price of one, and they included these juices.' Elena could have seen this as a nice gesture from her father to her mother, maybe even a romantic one. Perhaps she could have advised them that they should stop eating that kind of food since it was not good for their health, but that they should enjoy it now. But, no, Elena got angry!

'How can you eat a takeaway for breakfast?!' she yelled at them. 'Don't you see that you're poisoning yourselves? Dad, do you want Mum to die?'

Her parents didn't understand Elena's anger, so they downplayed it, tried to make a joke of it, but this only increased her fury. 'How can you think this is funny? How is this not important to you?' The argument continued for a while, to the point where Elena reproached them for never having taken good care of her. She told them that it was lucky she discovered on her own how to look after herself, because if it had been up to them, who knows how she would be now? She took her son and went out into the street feeling devastated, her blood boiling, her chest and stomach clenched, and crying out of frustration.

These kinds of arguments started to become more frequent, and they always ended with Elena feeling misunderstood, alone, frustrated and upset at the things she had said. Sometimes even her parents ended up crying and apologising for being such 'bad parents'.

Can you see what was happening to Elena? Have you experienced something similar with your parents? It is obvious that she was concerned about them, but what was it that led her to react in that way? To not be able to bear seeing her parents hurting themselves, and yet also not being able to bear hurting them by yelling at them?

We can see that this is about control. It's about having to let go of control over other people and instead being there for them with love, understanding and advice, knowing that they have responsibility for their own bad decisions. That is their prerogative. We have to accept it. But, how come we can let go of control and accept certain people's choices and behaviours, but not others? We can understand logically that we have to respect other people's choices, but there is an ingredient here that messes up our good intentions, and, again, it is fear. If you are scared of the consequences of those specific choices, you feel the need to act because you are too scared to let go of control and put your pain in their hands.

Elena was afraid – terribly and immensely afraid. She was terrified at the thought of her parents dying. She was terrified of feeling unprotected. *How can they take care of me if they can't even take care of themselves?* Parents are supposed to be the ultimate protectors; they are our roots, our foundation, our ultimate refuge, and feeling that this refuge was fragile, ignorant and weak made Elena feel vulnerable. She was terrified of living without protection and terrified that if something happened to her parents, she would be left alone. So every word that came out of her mouth was laden with fear, insecurity, loneliness and fragility, and her heart broke further when she saw how much she was making her parents suffer, whom she loved so much.

Being scared internally has a tremendous impact on all our relationships. There can be no relationship that is completely healthy and based on pure love if we love or care from a place of fear. This can happen when we fear that the other person can't meet all our expectations and mirrors back to us what we lack, or because we want to be very close to them so as to not risk losing them. We may want to take care of those we love to make sure they love us back, or make sure they are okay so that we are okay. We may not be completely honest in our conversations and never fully open up due to fear of not being liked or making a mistake, or being hurt, or being so vulnerable that we lose control of the situation.

Some people are lucky enough to find a friend or a person who can act as a shoulder to cry on, someone with whom they can open up and be themselves. Talking to someone like this can give you the first tools to heal yourself. Others go to therapy, which can also help, but you will only truly heal if you manage to fill yourself with love. And when I say love, I mean true love, pure love. That feeling of admiration for every detail of life, which makes you feel grateful and full, and makes you breathe deeply when you realise that you are feeling it. The more love you feel, the less fear you have, and the more fear you have, the less able you are to feel love. Love is trusting, letting go, surrendering and admiring life for what it is.

Labels

Expectations are a great enemy that we constantly face. From a young age, we are taught how the world works – how to love; how to relate to others; how to coexist; what is right and what is wrong. We are given two polar opposite categories for most things in life: what is considered good and what is considered bad. We are taught to stay in the realm of the good, and to always reject anything that represents the bad.

Although it is obvious to each of us what belongs in which group, we each have a personalised list in our own minds, which may differ from other people's – even that of our closest friends, or siblings we shared a household with, but especially those who may have had a different education to us or grew up in another culture. Wherever we were raised, in whatever circumstances, we cling to our list of what is good and what is bad, and accept it as the absolute truth.

We spend our lives trying to be on the side of good, feeling guilty every time we cross over to the supposed bad side, repenting for it and blaming those who made us cross over. We are told that defending our values is honourable, that we must fight against the bad. In some religions, we are even told that if we do a 'bad' thing we could be punished for eternity.

So this means we spend our lives judging everything and everyone, including ourselves, while carrying a lot of labels around with us, ready to apply them. The main ones say 'GOOD' or 'BAD', and so, to every act we witness, every conversation we have, every person we meet, every moment we experience, we attach one of these labels. It is sunny today: GOOD. It is raining: BAD. There is traffic: BAD. The waitress smiled at me: GOOD. My child is not doing their homework: BAD. He is polite: GOOD. My partner has given me a gift: GOOD. But they didn't share with me that they had an argument with their parents: BAD. And so we go through each day – *this is good, this is bad, this is good, this is bad* – without fully realising that our only reference for deciding if something belongs on one side or the other is what we have been taught.

The fact is, nobody has the exact same references as us. In the same circumstances, some will apply the label 'GOOD' and others the label 'BAD'. And so we spend our lives fighting among ourselves, not understanding how something so obviously good or bad to us can be the opposite to someone else. We can accept that someone may not attach the same labels to something as we do when that person is not close to us – we accept it as part of life – but what happens when that person is someone we love, or rather, someone we need to love us – and by this I mean someone who takes care of us, who understands us, who protects us, who knows us, who gives us what we need – does not attach the same labels as we do?

Your partner wants to go out with their friends, but you see that as a bad thing. You want them to take you along, or to want to go out with you instead. Your partner wants you to understand that they love you even though they sometimes prefer to hang out with their friends.

Your children don't try hard enough in school, and you see this as a problem. They see school as pointless and difficult.

Your friends behave in a way that you find objectionable – you don't like how they raise their children, how much they drink or how they dress. They think it's okay, but you don't …

Good or Bad?

There are countless disagreements caused by these discrepancies in what we consider good or bad, right or wrong. And it wouldn't be a problem if it didn't bring two enormous problems along with it.

The first is that we, of course, need to feel that we are happy, that we are loved and that we are doing things well in order to feel fulfilled. And if we feel that things in our lives are not going as they should, we feel like we have a 'bad' life, and that makes us feel insecure, guilty and, above all, afraid ... of doing things wrong. Constantly trying to live up to our expectations of ourselves is one of our greatest challenges in life.

The other problem is that we base all of our happiness on what happens outside of us – on whether our job, our children, ourselves and the people who are supposed to love us can fulfil our expectations. How often do you feel like a bad daughter, a bad mother, a bad partner, a bad friend, a bad citizen, a bad human being, because you haven't done something in the way that you think is 'right', or because you didn't know how to do something you felt you should know how to do well? 'I can't control my kids. I don't know how to communicate with my partner. I haven't called my friends.' All these things we label as 'wrong' or 'bad'.

One of our biggest problems is our reliance on everything and everyone in our life being 'good' in order to feel satisfied and happy. In other words, our wellbeing and sense of peace depend on things going 'well' on the outside – or rather, on what we understand as going 'well'.

And yet, how can we leave our happiness – something so relative and subjective – in the hands of something outside of ourselves? I'm not talking about momentary happiness here; I'm talking about the overall enjoyment and satisfaction we get from our life. For most of us, that kind of happiness depends on how much the external world aligns with what we've been taught as 'good' and 'right', and it means we feel a desperate need to control it.

Control

As we cannot allow things to happen on their own, by chance, and risk them not going well, we want to control everything. After all, we need to make sure that we are heading towards what will make us happy, which, as we know, is supposed to be the ideal – our idea of what is 'right'. That might be the perfect life partner, model children, a fulfilling job, a cosy house, beauty, health, true friendships. We drive ourselves crazy trying to control all these factors – or rather, making ourselves believe that we can control them. We want to impose order and predictability on everything in our lives, from the deepest thing to the most superficial.

For example, what clothes are on trend right now? It's important to know what's in fashion and what's not because we have to look beautiful to please ourselves and others. We have to control what our children do, because, of course, we have to be good mothers, and that involves having intelligent, responsible, happy children who like nature and eat everything. We can't have children who don't dutifully do their homework, who don't say hello, who are noisy and lazy – that's definitely not 'right'. So we make an enormous effort to make sure everything turns out well for us, and if we come up against something we don't like, we can often fly off the handle. 'I can't believe you haven't done your homework!' 'How could you lie to me?' 'What have you done? This isn't like you!' 'You can't be stuck inside the house all day – you need to get some fresh air!'

If something escapes our control, we feel terrible. If we haven't gone to the gym, we beat ourselves up: *I haven't exercised, I'm lazy* ... If we don't feel like going out and talking to people, we think, *But I have to do it, it's the right thing to do*, so we force ourselves to go out. On we struggle, and for what? To stay in that place of 'goodness', where we are doing what is right, and to distance ourselves as much as we can from the place that is 'bad' ... because we don't want to go there. And if we feel like we are there, it creates problems for us. We complain, we get depressed, we give up, we isolate ourselves, we lose motivation. How exhausting this all is! If only we could stop judging everything and relinquish just a little of that control.

Embracing the unknown

Another factor comes into all of this, and that is fear of the unknown. We're terrified of not knowing what or who we're facing, so in any new situation we immediately look for similarities with previous situations we've experienced to help guide us on how to act. When we meet someone new, our brain immediately starts searching through our mental archives for similarities with someone we already know. If we think, *Oh, this person reminds me of so-and-so*, in some way we start approaching them as if they were so-and-so. We might try a new restaurant, because, 'Look, it has the same decor as that other restaurant we like, and the food is very similar.' We look for familiar ground, because we feel we cannot afford to be completely ignorant of how to deal with a situation. When we move to a new city, if we don't find something that reminds us of a place where we used to live, we become very destabilised. We need a neighbourhood that reminds us of something from our past – perhaps a coffee shop like the one we used to go to, or people to relate to like the ones we've met before. We are not capable of enjoying completely unknown territory, because what we do not know, we can't control. Because we haven't labelled it yet, we don't know who to be in the face of it, and that frightens us.

This means that if you suddenly find yourself in a new place, a new job, or with people who are completely unknown to you, and you look for similarities and don't find them, you will immediately feel unstable and fearful. You might even reject them without giving them a chance.

Has this ever happened to you? It's such a shame that we can't face the new and unknown with open arms and an open heart, without judging, without controlling, just simply observing and letting ourselves be carried away by the situation, to see how we behave in the face of this new thing. Instead, we tend to hold on to the first thing we find that resembles something we already know.

We have no idea how we would respond to something we've never faced before. It might, in fact, lead to a wonderful experience! But, of course, letting ourselves be carried away so freely, so joyfully, would mean having to break out of the shell we have created around ourselves and act from an open heart – and we can't risk that, because we're too afraid of suffering.

I promise you that when you connect to your heart, you are not controlled any more by the brain's fears. It opens in you a trust, a knowing, a sensation of strength and light, and you start embracing the unknown and welcoming what comes your way, because you're not alone any more. You feel so full and calm that you don't need to control the outcomes or prevent the different possible scenarios from happening.

Good or Bad?

Reflection: Lose your memories

We need to practise the habit of 'erasing' our memories. Yes, you heard me – it's an amazing skill to have. We should try to do it with people, places and situations. It would force us to step into our authentic self, instead of our learnt self.

Next time, when you meet someone you have a history with – maybe a colleague, another parent at school, your partner – approach the encounter with no memory, no past history whatsoever between you, and see how you feel.

When we do this, our head is taken out of the equation. There is no judgement at all, we just approach the situation authentically and that gives the encounter a completely different dimension. If we don't remember what that person did or didn't do to us, we will embrace in that moment whatever they are bringing to the table, and this will be received with no preconceptions, because we won't remember what we thought was good or bad, right or wrong.

The next time you go on the tube or drive around your area, look around with no memories. You will immediately appreciate things for what they are and face everything – the architecture, the trees, the lights, the noises, the colours, the signs, everything – as if it is the first time you are seeing them. That takes you immediately to the present moment. Not only will it relax you right away (as it could be taken as a mindfulness exercise, too), but it will give you the sensation of gratitude because you will be grateful to be able to see and experience so many things.

Look at your kids afresh next time you see them, with no memory of their flaws. You will see that only love will come from you ... and they will perceive it. They will even ask, 'Why are you looking at me like that?' with a smile on their face.

What I want you to achieve with this reflection is to remove all your learnt judgements and to be authentic in any situation or in front of any person. It's really difficult to do, as our brain needs to prevent us from doing this; it needs to remind us of our past, raise alerts, point out signs, but if you do it little by little, one situation at a time, you will start feeling the difference ... and the benefits.

You have nothing to lose by trying. You might feel unprotected, but the risk is worth it, because this way of living is contagious. You can help others do it, too, by just approaching them with no memory and therefore no judgement.

I heard a story of a mum who started to practise this every time she took her child to chemotherapy sessions. Until then, every session had been a nightmare; she felt so weighed down every time she crossed the threshold of that hospital. So she started trying to approach each visit as if it were her first time. And guess what? She started noticing the children's drawings on the walls, all the beautiful details that were in the lively and colourful paintings. She relaxed her face, her body language changed, and her child felt it. The mum felt lighter; not happier, but more accepting, more positive, without the weight of all the past sessions, without the weight of her fears for the future. Of course, that was all still in her, but she tried not to pay attention to it, and instead

Good or Bad?

just embraced every minute with her child, as well as the kindness of the nurses and the compassion they had for the other children that were there.

Be mindful that the past and the future only exist if you bring them to your present. If you decide to embrace your present as it comes, as often as you can, you will start feeling the lightness you deserve.

CHAPTER 9
Where Are You?

'We can forgive a child who is afraid of the dark. The true tragedy of life is when a man is afraid of the light.'

– Plato

Many of us feel emotionally alone and misunderstood; often we can recognise that we don't even understand why ourselves. No one else really knows what is happening inside us. When we are with people, we don't tend to notice it so much. We work, talk, exercise, and we can temporarily forget the internal void that accompanies us wherever we go. It is very difficult for us to face it.

Then, suddenly, we are alone: in bed, with the lights off, before sleeping; in the shower; in the car. In those moments when we are truly alone, we have several options:

A. Our brain gets activated and we start thinking about a thousand things. Before sleeping, we might review the day, think about tomorrow, remember how bad something made us feel or how well or poorly we did. We think and overthink in order not to remain in silence.
B. We use an external element to distract us. The TV, our mobile phone or iPad, the radio, a book, music, podcasts . . . whatever keeps our mind occupied.
C. The last option for these moments is silence: that dark, empty and terrifying silence. Have you ever been in

silence? I don't just mean the absence of external noise, but also mental silence ... shhhh ... the silence that occurs when suddenly you turn off everything that can entertain your senses (sight, hearing, taste, touch, smell) and even turn off your thoughts. You just stay there, quiet, still, not thinking about anything, but paying attention to what is inside you. What is there? What do you feel? Is it strange? Try it. Just for a moment, close your eyes, take a deep breath and stay in mental silence ... shhhh ...

The first thing that usually happens when you try Option C, if you manage to do it, is that your mind starts to look for a place to settle, and when it can't find one, a thought comes to you. At that precise moment, you realise that a thought has come to you and you say to yourself, *Oh no, I shouldn't be thinking about anything!* And right there, my friend, is the key. Stay with that moment, and don't let it go; stay with the moment when that first thought comes to you and you become aware of it.

This is the first step towards healing all your pains, the first and absolutely necessary step to begin the healing process. Read on, and I will explain how.

Being in silence

One of the big problems we have is that we don't give ourselves these moments to be alone in silence. It's unbelievable – we don't have the time, and we don't want to either, so we don't seek these moments out. We don't find them because we have other priorities, other things to dedicate our time to in a more efficient way. And we're not used to it; we haven't learnt to be alone in internal silence. Perhaps in recent years we've thought more about it when hearing about meditation or yoga – after all, the basis of meditation is to achieve silence to connect with your true self. But maybe the idea of your true self sounds a little mystical, so let me put it in another way.

Let's go back to the moment when you tried to stop thinking and your mind started searching for a place to settle, and suddenly a thought came to you: *Oh, I can't control this*, or, *Oh, this is impossible, I can't stop my mind from whirring*. Whatever it was, the point is that at that moment you realised you had a thought. And earlier I said that was the key, but why? Well, because at that moment, the one who realised that a thought came up, that person, my dear, was YOU.

At that precise moment, you managed to differentiate between the brain that produced the thought and YOU, who realised you had the thought. The one who realised, that's your true self, the one you have to identify with, connect with and live with, because that's YOU. Thoughts are just your conscious mind working overtime. This realisation of YOU doesn't come from your conscious mind, it comes from a deeper awareness that you sense in the silence, when you quiet your thinking. The philosopher Rupert Spira has a metaphor that imagines 'YOU' as a screen in the movie theatre, and 'you' as the movie projected onto it. If you think you are the movie, you get all these emotions, stresses, troubles, from whatever movie is being projected onto the screen at that time, but when you realise you are the screen – still, calm, unaffected by the film, just witnessing it – then you find peace in the realisation that everything else is not YOU.

If it helps to locate your true self in a certain part of your body, just as we locate thoughts in our head, I suggest that the YOU who realises that you're thinking can be thought of as residing more around the heart or chest, but with a thread of light and energy that connects it to the mind, up through the neck. If you close your eyes and take a deep breath, you can direct your attention to that channel, which has its source in the chest and radiates up to the head through the neck. That YOU is there, encompassing that whole area, radiating through your whole body.

Your brain is like a computer; it's programmed to think, review, predict, imagine, retell your story, judge, doubt everything and compare. But YOU are the one who realised that your brain had a thought while you were trying to be mentally silent. To start healing and to begin your journey down the path to true happiness, you have to create moments when you're alone and can connect with YOURSELF.

At first, it's quite difficult. It's not easy to get to the silence where this awareness sits, as there is too much noise going on in our heads and outside us, but even if you only do it for a fraction of a second, that is good enough. It's simply about realising who YOU are and who your thinking brain is.

Behind the shield

We've talked before about how we all have a shield around, a wall we've built up between our raw heart and the outside world. That wall protects us, and we've built it based on pain and fear. When we're little girls, we don't have it – we're raw, pure, innocent – but as we experience painful things, we build up that protection. And there comes a point where it's fully constructed, and we become so accustomed to it that we believe it's a part of us.

Some of us say things like, 'I have a shield that's very difficult to break,' or, 'I don't open up to just anyone.' The reality is that we don't open up to ourselves, either. We're not truly aware of what's behind that shield or what it's made of, but that's where we live our lives from; our feelings and fears settle on that firm surface, and we think that's the foundation.

But it's not. The foundation is on the other side of that shield. That's where our true feelings lie, protected and out of reach to anyone, even ourselves. In fact, it's not really 'feelings' that are there; it's ONE feeling, just one, and that is LOVE.

The pure love we have as little girls gradually gets dented over time, and so we start covering it up to protect it from further damage. By the time we're grown up, it's completely hidden. So when we think we're feeling love, it's not true love; it's a kind of love that our brain creates based on judgements about who we are and what's in front of us.

But your true self, the one that is pure love, pure peace, is still there. It has been intact ever since you were born. That's why identifying it is so important. Opening the little door or a window to that peaceful environment behind your shield, where YOU are, that's the key.

Accessing love

What is my main objective here? I want you to be able to access that love, so that you can start living from it, because I know that only then can you truly be happy. Only then can you truly love and allow yourself to be loved.

There are two main ways to access that love: one is from within; the other is from without. Whether you do it from within or without, it can be quite intense, because you have to break down that shell that you've built on pain, and of course by breaking it you will see each of the pieces that formed it.

Where Are You?

But at the same time, it is beautiful and very inspiring to realise who you are without fears, without prejudices, and with calm.

To break the shell from the outside, a big impact is needed. And even with a big impact, it may be that only a piece of the shell is broken. Feeling that a piece of that wall, which protects us, is broken leads us immediately to feel fear – the most absolute terror we have ever known. It will depend on us whether we then dare to break the shell completely or patch it up and rebuild it.

What external things can break our shell? Things so big that we are totally overwhelmed, and our brain is not able to process them. Things like the death of a loved one. When someone close to us dies, someone we are connected to from the soul – a child, a father, a mother, a brother, a sister – the pain of that loss is so great that our armour cannot shield us from it; it reaches directly into our heart, which is as exposed as raw flesh. I don't know if you have lost someone so close, but if it has happened to you, you'll know what I'm talking about. The pain of the death of that person is so deep that we have nowhere to place it; it is immense and unbearable.

At the same time, a surprising thing happens. In the middle of that pain, sensations of deep calm, deep love, come over us – something we might find difficult to understand because they are mixed with so much sadness and anguish. But if you pay attention, you will recognise what I'm talking about, because in this pain, what we suddenly discover is our pure heart, which has been so abruptly exposed. This feeling is wonderfully terrifying.

As soon as it is exposed, the heart sends a signal through that channel I discussed earlier (see page 118) to our mind, and suddenly we wake up and realise that it is there. When we are in the midst of pain, normally we are not able to realise this pure well of love inside ourselves. If we were, how many secrets we would discover! We would see our essence so clearly. Like when a vase is broken and you can see the layers of what it's made of, we would see our beautiful essence, in all its peace, stillness and light. It can also happen when you have children. There are moments when the love you feel for your child is so great that the armour opens by itself, which is terrifying, so *snap!* We close it again and keep functioning with our conscious brain. But if something happens to our child – if they are on the brink of death or have an accident – the love and fear we feel is also large enough to break us – or rather the shell. That's right, it doesn't break us; it breaks the shell, leaving us fully exposed.

And then what happens? Well, it might be that we can use those moments to finally remove the armour once and for all. We can realise that this openness only leads to profound love. Yes, you are deeply loving the person you lost, you are deeply loving your newborn child ... and when you really feel these things, nothing except that love exists in the world – or at least nothing else is that important. Suddenly nothing else seems quite so urgent or even problematic.

A close friend of mine once told me that after a routine mammogram, she had an 'a-ha' moment like this. The doctor told her that they had seen a shadow on one of her breasts and he wanted to repeat the test just in case. So, she went back to the room and had the test repeated. While waiting for the results, she panicked. It was the first time something like this had happened to her – she was healthy, quite young, and a very busy and successful woman, but suddenly she was waiting in a room, alone, unexpectedly, to hear whether she had a lump on her breast, which might mean cancer.

Where Are You?

But in that waiting room something magical happened. My friend became aware that at the same time, while she was panicking, she also felt peace. She told me she hadn't felt that peaceful for a long, long time. Suddenly, all her duties ceased to feel important; all her daily worries – about her job, her home, her kids, her partner – dissipated, and all she could think about was how scared she was of having to face cancer. For a second, she said, she even wished for the results of the mammogram to be positive, as that would mean having to stop all she was doing and only focus on one thing: healing.

She thought she was crazy, wishing for that outcome – it seemed somehow outrageous. With an emotional smile I told her that she had discovered the secret. The moment she had heard the news of her potential cancer, it had impacted her shield and broken it, leaving her open and vulnerable. The worries and expectations of her mind had suddenly evaporated and all she could feel was love for life and for her family, and with that she had found peace.

Fortunately, it was a false alarm and she was given a clean bill of health, but the experience helped her realise that her mind was playing a very dangerous game with her in daily life, as she was caught up with everything being perfect, efficient and 'good'. After that moment she started living more from that place of peace she had discovered. Her life became slower and she became more present with people – no rushing to the next thing any more or expecting perfection from everyone. She realised that even the worst scenario can bring peace and love, so she let go of control and wasn't scared any more. Now, she is extremely spiritual, and we often enjoy long, deep conversations about the meaning of life, the uniqueness of loving and the compassion we feel for people who are still struggling, being led through life by their minds, without knowing that being led by the heart completely changes the experience.

This is what can happen to any of us. Isn't it beautiful?

The other option – the safer, more controlled option – is to break the shell little by little from within, without a big impact from the outside. Only YOU can break it ... and in fact you can do more than break it. You can utterly disintegrate it.

As we've discussed, that shell is our protection, part of the identity we have created based on the image we've developed of ourselves since birth, based on our learnt beliefs of how we should be or act. Perhaps we have even built an identity that is the opposite of what we experienced at home out of pure rebellion or the need to survive.

The thing is, this identity is constructed, it is not an authentic identity. If we can first recognise and then connect with our true identity, it will gradually strengthen from within and gain ground over that false identity; it will grow and gain control over everything, so gradually the shell disintegrates as we realise that we are incredibly strong, leaving our soul completely exposed.

This requires a lot of courage. It requires making the decision to do it, as well as time and patience. We can notice it happening by observing ourselves at a moment when something makes us feel very emotional. If we see something beautiful on TV, for example, a love story in a movie, or a performance that touches our soul, first, we might connect with what we are seeing, then a strong, dry knot can form in our throat, which gradually descends to our chest, and, if we let it, it reaches our heart and tears come out. That is what happens when we have a glimpse that a window is opening in the shell from within. Tears come out as a reaction to the freedom of love that we are feeling at that moment, which reminds us deep inside of the freedom of love that we felt when we were little. When we get emotional, we cry, and sometimes it's not because we're sad, it's because we're happy. It's because we're in love, it's because we're releasing the strength that we constantly exert inside to try to keep our shell intact.

I like to use the example of a soldier and their armour. Imagine a pure, beautiful, capable and intelligent girl. She has been told since birth that she has to go to war, to win battle after battle, and she is being prepared for all the fights she will have to face. She sees the wars, the battles, the bombs falling on all sides, so she uses the tools she has developed and the knowledge she has been taught to build her armour. Every time she is wounded, she designs an even more effective and modern suit of armour, with all the intricate details. She learns what things can hurt her and predicts what may happen, so she adds more and more gadgets and protections to her armour. She continues to walk around with the armour on, and also collects weapons so that she may attack whenever she needs to. Each time the armour weighs more, but of course she cannot afford to take it off because there are minefields constantly in her path. From time to time, she stops to listen to the battles going on around her and feels how everyone is also building their armour as best they can, too. They start to relate to each other armour to armour, rather than person to person ... Imagine them all, encased in metal, shiny, strong and heavy. But, of course, no one knows who anyone really is, because they are all relating to their armour. No one ever dares to shed the armour and expose themselves to all the dangers – they feel too fragile, unable to face the battles without it. Bombs and gunshots are constantly going off around them, and most of them do not even consider whether they could survive without their armour because that option has never existed. Since they were born, they have been taught how to protect themselves, how to attack and how to advance through life without getting hurt.

I love this metaphor because it sums up very well the way we live. The only things that can rid us of our armour are either a very strong blow from the outside, which pierces through the sturdy metal and hits our body, or for us to decide little by little to remove the weight of the armour plates that we carry around with us.

The fact is that no one has told us that all the shootings and bomb blasts come from other people's armour. And no one has told us that without the armour we are in fact invincible and immortal, that we radiate a beautiful light, which in itself shields us from any harm. And when something bad comes to us, and crosses through that light we emanate, it transforms into something beautiful and good, and even reflects light back out, to change the source of whatever that bad thing was.

So, yes, we can be hurt, but every time we expose ourselves to this pain without wearing any armour, that pain strengthens us because it doesn't kill us. Yes, we have that superpower – we have the ability to manipulate pain and turn it into power by feeling that it really hurts, while knowing that it fades away. And when we do this, little by little we lose the fear of being hurt, because we realise that nothing can defeat us. As we realise this, we can finally dare to take off our armour, because we no longer fear anything.

We don't go through this process from the head, which is where the armour is manufactured in the first place, but from the heart, which is our true self. And we will only achieve it if we are finally able to realise who we are and what we are capable of, in our essence.

Let's find out how.

Where Are You?

Reflection: Find your silence

As an actress, I've had the pleasure of incarnating various different roles – the bad guy, the arms dealer, the nice girl. None of these characters are me, and yet I have to be them, think like them, feel like them, move like them, react and respond like them. I have their past story in my head, even in my body: their dreams of the future, their goals ... I become them any time I hear the word 'Action!' During those moments I am not me – I shout, I cry, I feel fear – but I, Lorena, am still intact. I am quiet, in there somewhere, still, silent, not intervening at all in what this character is feeling, saying or doing. I don't judge, I don't say anything to them, I just witness whatever is going on for them. Only when I hear 'Aaaaand ... cut!' do I awaken and go back to being me.

I want you to try something similar in this reflection. Imagine you are inhabiting a character, who has all the characteristics that you have, so that you are totally lost in that role: reacting like you, feeling like you, being you ...

Now, try to locate where your true self would be, the 'actress' who is behind that character, sitting in silence, witnessing your performance ... Now imagine you hear the words 'Aaaaand cut!' and you stop being you, to become YOU, connecting to the calm awareness that is there inside.

Pause what you're doing for a second, breathe in, breathe out, and stop being you for a bit. Just sit still.

It Starts With You

You might feel an emptiness around you and a calm inside you that is magical ... You might even struggle to get thoughts coming to your head ... That is your pure essence. All the rest is just your performance, using the script you have learnt and the character you have created for yourself. The more you can get to that point of silence, the more you will start loving and embracing it, and finally you will meet YOURSELF there, and you can start recognising who that is, how she is, what she wants, what her dreams and her purpose are ... The more you are (with) her, the more you will want to be (with) her, and gradually you will reduce the time you spend being in character.

CHAPTER 10
Your Reflection

'The only way to truly see yourself is in the reflection of someone else's eyes.'

– Voltaire

Have you ever thought about what you ask of others, about what you expect from them? What do you like and dislike about the people you know? It's a really cool exercise to do. So, just off the top of your head, think about what you expect from your mother. You might say love, understanding and support. From your partner? Love, understanding, support, appreciation, physical attraction and liking you as a person. From your boss? Recognition for your work and an appreciation for how good you are. From your friends? You want them to love you despite everything, listen to you, be loyal and for you to have fun together. From your children? You want them to love you, respect you, appreciate you and admire you.

Have you noticed that we expect more or less the same things from all the people around us? And what happens when we don't get what we expect from them? Basically, we feel pain, be it sadness, frustration or disappointment. I would go further and say fear, too, because we expect these people who form the foundations of our lives, who provide our support system, to give us the very things that will keep us safe, stable and well.

Now, let's look at how we judge the people around us. We might say, 'I can't stand it when he does this,' or, 'I can't deal with her when she does that, she's so annoying,' about certain people.

Have you ever stopped to think about what you like and don't like about other people? There are usually some common traits that we don't like in others. We might not like it when people talk too much, or the way they talk, or when they have a certain attitude. We might not like one friend because she always complains, or that our mother is always scared of everything, or that our son is not tidy or responsible. We might not like that our partner is easily distracted, or when people are uneducated or ignorant or don't share our values . . .

I'm not talking about superficial preferences here, I'm talking about the things that make us feel really uncomfortable inside, the things we can't stand, which we would change without a second thought if we could. What's going on with those things? Why don't we like them? Simply put, we don't like them because of how they make us feel. But why should we let how another person lives their life affect us? Well, studies have shown that what we can't stand in others puts right in front of us what we're afraid of in ourselves. Like it or not, that's how it is. It has nothing to do with the other person, it's all about our own fears.

I had a friend many years ago, whom I gradually lost touch with, but for a time we were very close. I loved being around her; we laughed a lot, talked a lot, she was very sweet, slow and calm, and that was lovely because it made me feel peaceful when I was with her. We could spend hours talking and drinking coffee. One day, we had the opportunity to go to the mountains and ski, so we went on a trip with some other friends. She and I were good at skiing, but we had never tried snowboarding, so that day we decided to give it a try. We hired an instructor, rented snowboards and headed up the mountain on the ski lift to learn this new sport.

That day was a turning point in our friendship. We fell many times while trying to learn, and every time she fell, it took her forever to get back up. She would complain about how she couldn't do it: her wrists hurt, her butt hurt, her boots wouldn't latch on to the board, she couldn't do it, over and over again ... and I became increasingly annoyed. At first, I took it calmly and encouraged her to get up and try again, but there came a point where I couldn't take it any more. I couldn't stand her complaints, her fragility, the way she lacked the strength to say, 'Okay, I'll get up and try again.' I was boiling with anger every time I heard her say, 'I can't,' or 'Ouch,' and every time her tears came... I couldn't bear it! She was interrupting the whole class because we had to wait an eternity for her to get back up again every time, and it slowed me down and made me unable to fully enjoy my experience. But my body was reacting to something else. How could it be that I felt this annoyance in every cell of my body every time she complained? The truth is, I was disgusted by her weakness.

That weekend changed the way I saw her – that ability she had to be calm and pause I began to see as passivity, laziness, a lack of will or motivation, fragility, and I didn't like it. I never saw her the same way again.

What do you think happened to me? Of course, I was unconsciously seeing something in front of me that I had always fought against and could never accept in myself – weakness. I always tried again, nothing could defeat me, I was strong, I always solved things. Clearly, it was an internal struggle that I had with myself, in which I neutralised any hint of fragility.

It Starts With You

This is just a very clear example of how we cannot stand something in another person that reflects something about ourselves that we avoid, fight against, don't like or are afraid of.

In summary, almost all of our daily life is based on what we expect from others and the constant judgements we make of every person we encounter. *This person is nice, this person is not. This person is a bit weird but nice. This person is too friendly; it makes me nervous. This person didn't ask me how I'm doing; does she not care? She only cares about herself, how selfish. This person is nice – what a beautiful thing she did. This person is rude – she didn't even say thank you!* And so, we live our whole lives this way, day in, day out, judging others, confirming our beliefs based on what we see in them, and rejecting certain ways of being ourselves.

Of course, since everyone lives this way, we're not surprised at it, and we don't know that there's another way of living. But there is hope, because we don't like being like this. We complain about people judging us, and about not being able to be ourselves. We complain about having to follow certain standards. The discomfort we feel at living this way, even if it's hidden very deep down, is there, and that's what opens the window of hope for us to change and to start living for ourselves, not through other people's opinions of us.

We have talked about how we always expect things from others. To a greater or lesser extent, it's as if we carry a ball in our hand and throw it to anyone we see, hoping they will throw it back to us in the same way – with the same force, direction and movement. Well, believe me, you don't need to carry a ball, and you don't need to expect anything from anyone. Instead of looking at someone and waiting for them to give us what we want, we can give ourselves everything we want. And there will come a time when we won't even need those things from ourselves any more, because we will have become those qualities we seek.

I'm going to explain.

Generally, what we expect from others is love, affection, understanding, to be valued, to be listened to, to be seen and to be liked. That's it, in a nutshell. So let me ask you a question. Do you give yourself all those things? Do you give yourself love? Do you understand yourself? Do you value yourself? Do you listen to yourself? Do you see yourself?

I've been seeing phrases such as 'love yourself' and 'value yourself' a lot lately, but this is easier said than done, so sometimes these just seem like empty words. I think it's very important to explain what it means to love yourself, what it means to value yourself, listen to yourself or see yourself. Because we're not talking about going to a spa or using luxury creams or any of those other things that would fall under the concept of 'self-care'. It's something complex, but at the same time very simple.

Basically, inside of you are your two selves, right? There's you and there's YOU. The former resides in your brain, and the latter, as I said before, lives in your heart, which is connected to your mind (see pages 118 – 119). When we tried the reflection of finding our silence (see page 127), we noticed that when a thought came to us, the one who thought the thought was you, and the one who realised you'd had the thought was YOU.

It's not that we have a split personality or anything like that, although there are moments when it might feel like it, because we hear conversations in our heads like, 'I don't even know what I want', 'I tell myself no, but I end up doing it', 'I start off very motivated but I give up so easily, even though

I really want it!' ... These contradictions are part of the identity you have built for yourself – or rather, the identity you have built based on your experiences and life events. This is the you that keeps itself alive by bouncing the ball; it's the autopilot computer in your brain that is designed with sublime intelligence to adapt to the environment you live in, teaching you how to behave, to compare yourself to others and to construct yourself accordingly. This version of you is always active, constantly needing to notice itself, confirm its beliefs and control everything all the time.

The other you is the real YOU, the one who hasn't changed a bit in your whole life. The one you remember from when you were a child. That YOU doesn't age, doesn't change shape, because it is YOU in essence. Take a moment to observe your thoughts ... you're aware of the thoughts themselves, but what happens between thought and thought? That nanosecond of silence, that fraction of consciousness in between thoughts, which is a witness to everything that happens behind your eyes and in your mind, that's YOU.

This other YOU is love, wisdom and security. It doesn't need stimulation, it doesn't need to compare itself to anyone, it just is. It loves, it exists, without problems, without guilt, without fears, without searching for anything. It is pure relaxation, pure calm, pure stillness. And it always accompanies you, because it is YOU.

Both versions are in your mind, all the time, and my main goal in this book is for you to locate YOURSELF, to realise that YOU have yourself and that, little by little, YOU will direct your life, shed your armour and live based on who YOU are, without needing anything from anyone, so that every relationship you decide to have, every step you decide to take, is based on desire, on wanting, never on need.

Your Reflection

Finding YOU

You know, the first thing to realise is that YOU are there, with yourself always, witnessing everything you think, everything you see, every decision you make. Once you realise this and know that you can separate your thoughts from YOURSELF, the next step is to get to know YOU, to connect with YOU, by plugging your consciousness into YOURSELF.

To do this, it is ideal to spend time alone, in silence, in calm. You don't need to meditate if you don't feel like it or don't know how, just being alone is enough. In the car, on the bus, at home, in the shower, when you close your eyes before going to sleep... YOU are with YOURSELF.

There are many reflections you can try to establish that relationship with YOURSELF. Here are a couple of examples below.

Reflection: Liking yourself

With your eyes closed, focus on the sensation in your chest. Breathe and scan yourself. Take a tour of each part of your body and remember anecdotes and experiences you've had with your body. Running, falling, dancing ... Share these stories with YOURSELF as if you were talking to your best friend, your confidante – a faithful companion or soul sister to whom you can tell absolutely everything. Tell YOURSELF inwardly, 'What a beautiful body you have,' or 'I love your belly.' Remember when you had your children, or, if you don't have children, remember any other changes your body may have been through. Say, 'I love your face, you're beautiful.' Say it with all the love and sincerity in the world.

What happened? If you were able to do this well and verbalise in silence the love you feel for your body, congratulations. It's wonderful that you can appreciate yourself, without witnesses, without anyone hearing you, just YOU with YOURSELF, expressing how beautiful you are and how grateful you are to have yourself.

But what if you couldn't manage it? Unfortunately, the first time we try to do this, the vast majority of us find it very difficult. We feel like we're lying to ourselves. We think, *Why should I say, 'I like your belly,' if I really hate it and can't wait to get rid of it?* For many of us, it's very difficult to say, 'How pretty you are,' because we don't believe we're pretty and so it's uncomfortable for us to say it.

It's terrible that we can't like ourselves! Something so basic, so pure and beautiful, and yet we can't do it! But how can we expect to be liked by others if we don't like ourselves? How are we going to let go of the need to be liked by others if we ourselves, who are the only thing we really have, don't like ourselves?

To combat this, we need to stop striving for an ideal self, as any ideal is basically made up of comparisons with others, or the judgements of others, or our expectations of perfection. It's difficult to value and like ourselves if we have an ideal in our minds that we will never be able to reach. Yes, it's nice to have a goal, a direction, but only when our vehicle is fully ready to take that trip towards it.

We should learn from how we appreciate other species in nature. Trees, for example – they are all just perfect as they are, aren't they? Straight or bent, tall or short, leafy or not, they are magnificent. They do their thing in peace, at their own pace; they grow, they give shelter to birds, they give fruits, they give shade ... Some last longer than others, some are bushes, some are oaks, but they all give oxygen. A bonsai, an apple tree ... it doesn't matter. Even when we decorate a pine tree for Christmas, we're not saying that the tree is not beautiful as it is and trying to cover its flaws, we are just having fun. We need to learn from that. We need to realise that we, too, are perfect as we are, in our essence. And yes, we are fortunate to be able to move, to change some things, to have fun decorating ourselves with clothes or make-up, but it shouldn't be because we feel we are faulty or not enough; it should be in gratitude at being able to have fun experiencing our body.

Let's try another reflection. This one is a bit more intense, so if you can't do it now, wait until you have at least five minutes where you are calm enough to do it.

Reflection: Revisit your inner child

Close your eyes and transport yourself to a painful moment in your childhood – the most painful one you can remember right now – without fear or pressure; it's just a memory. It may have been that day when you felt abandoned by your mother or father, the day you were hurt or somehow abused, or the day you witnessed something that hurt a lot. That moment when someone yelled at you, or didn't understand you, or laughed at you. Whatever it is, it will be something that happened to you as a child that caused you pain. I can tell you right now that it's common for it still to hurt in adulthood when you think about that moment, even though it's not happening any more. Just thinking about it produces pain.

I'm going to ask you to transport yourself there, with your eyes closed. Breathe and teleport yourself to that moment. As if you were a being of energy and light, full of love and calm, fly to your younger self and position yourself just behind your child's eyes. Observe what happens. Observe what that child sees, on the ground, to the sides, in front of them. Observe what that child is hearing and smelling. Observe what that child is feeling. Stay there for a while, observing from the perspective of your adult self, whose energy is currently inside the child. When you notice that the child feels bad, speak to her. Say to her, 'It's okay, you'll be okay.' Fill yourself with love and calmness, and smile. Whisper to her from inside, 'I'm you, I've come from the future, and I know you'll be okay. You'll continue with your life and you'll be an amazing woman.' Speak words full of love. Say to yourself, 'I love you, I adore you, stay calm.' Say to yourself above all, 'It's not your fault. You're a precious and pure child who is going through this, but it's not your fault. Forgive them – they are fragile and don't realise the magnitude of what they're doing.'

Love yourself, comfort yourself – your adult self to your child self. Stay there for a while, protecting and hugging yourself, while experiencing what happened to you as a movie. Fill yourself with self-love. When you feel that love, in that same dream, stand in front of your child self, look into her eyes and say, 'Sometimes I blamed you for this; I thought you could have done better or that you were too fragile, because it hurt me that you went

Your Reflection

through this, but you're beautiful and not at fault for anything. I forgive myself for blaming you and for feeling guilty. This is just something you had to experience, but believe me, you and I are much more than this, you'll see. I'm here. I love you with all my heart. Come with me – we're going to be amazing.' Then take her by the hand and return to the present moment. Now, open your eyes, breathe and observe how you feel.

This is a beautiful exercise, in which you are alone, with yourself, without witnesses, without anyone to tell or explain anything to. Allow yourself to go there and love yourself, forgive yourself, protect yourself, embrace yourself and smile at yourself. It's you, just you, so be brave, try it and let yourself go.

There are many circumstances you can apply these exercises to. And the more you do that, the more you will realise how important you are to yourself. For example, when you are alone with yourself, not sure how you are feeling or why, think back to when you were a little girl – how would she feel? Remember her way of thinking. When you are doing an activity you used to enjoy as a child, become her. Look yourself in the eye in a mirror, get up close, and look beyond your eyes. See your subtle sadness, remember your childhood dreams, smile at yourself and whisper, 'I love you,' remembering all you have been through.

Remember past experiences in which only you knew how you felt, and tell yourself about them. Tell yourself those secrets you have never shared with anyone – dare to verbalise them with your inner voice. You will find that you always have your best friend, your protective soul sister, within you, who doesn't judge anything you do and is always there for you. Talk to her all the time, in silence, without rushing. Don't be afraid to open up completely – she knows everything already.

It Starts With You

Earlier, I asked you to think about what you expect and ask for from others – your friends, your parents, your partner. Well, take that whole list of qualities and offer them to yourself. Like yourself, admire yourself, listen to yourself, value yourself, advise yourself – all with pure love, affection and understanding, and without pressure or demands.

For example, what would you say to your loving soul sister if she messed up something? You'd probably say something like, 'Don't worry, you didn't do it on purpose, it wasn't your intention, now we'll fix it.' Say that to yourself, with love and affection, and without blaming yourself. Dare to take those steps that are difficult for you – make fun of yourself sometimes, smile at yourself, say to yourself, 'You're so beautiful, I love you.' Say it from the heart, not from the head – from love, not from thought.

The more you say it to yourself, the easier it will be for you to say it and believe it, until there comes a time when that knowledge is already there, when you already have your constant companion within you, the one who gives you absolutely everything you need. And at that stage you're done – you don't need anything from anyone. And if you do still feel like you need something, you can think about what it is and give it to yourself.

For example, if you still feel like you need someone else to value something you've done well, you can reinforce that feeling of being valued yourself, by really telling yourself, 'You've done an amazing job. You've put in a lot of effort and achieved something incredible. I admire you, I value you, I love you.' You may even shed tears saying this to yourself and feeling it for real, because we truly melt when we feel loved.

The feeling you will achieve is the immense happiness and calmness of always feeling loved, valued, respected and heard

Your Reflection

in every moment. And what's even better is that YOU will have given all of that to yourself, the only one who truly knows you from the inside, the most important person in your life, the one who has been with you every second of your life, from the moment you were in your mother's womb to the moment you will die.

And you know what? Since you will already have what you need, you will let others be who they are and how they are. And if at any moment you want something from someone, you will ask for it from a place of emotional fullness, without fear that they won't give it to you, and without feeling the need to demand it. You will open your heart to receive love from others, understanding that everyone has their own life, their own path, and their own way of being and living.

CHAPTER 11
Love

*'Love is the ultimate meaning of everything around us.
It's not a mere sentiment; it is truth; it is the joy
that is at the root of all creation.'*

– Rabindranath Tagore

I once heard a psychologist say, 'If you're looking for your ideal partner, make a list of everything you want that person to have and how you want them to be. And once you have the list, become that person.'

I love this statement: you are the one who has to give yourself everything you need, and you are the one who will receive it all. There is nothing that makes us feel better than receiving love and giving love – and this way, you'll be doing both at the same time!

If you are able to do this, you're going to fill yourself with love. You're going to listen to yourself, talk to yourself, be patient with yourself, give yourself the best advice, have compassion for yourself, pamper yourself, take care of yourself, attend to yourself and encourage yourself. You will stop judging yourself, demanding things of yourself, controlling yourself, reducing yourself and rushing yourself through everything. You're going to fill yourself with love, by giving it all to yourself.

Love

And do you know what you will feel in return? Peace, pure peace. And at the same time, you will feel a wonderful strength, because you will open up. You will dare to show yourself as you are in every moment, because you will not judge yourself; instead, you will give yourself love, forgiveness and respect. And you will be able to extend that love you feel outwards, towards others.

You will feel stronger than ever, because you will have learnt to show yourself as you are, to expose yourself, to stay raw. Nothing about you will embarrass you, because you will have accepted yourself and therefore you will no longer be affected by the image of yourself that others may perceive, or by what they give or don't give you.

And when you have that love, respect and reassurance with you, constantly, wherever you go, whatever you do, you won't need anything or anyone. You won't be afraid of not being loved, because you already are – by the most important person in the world, the person who knows you best, who knows your deepest secrets and desires. You will feel full, at peace and without fear, and now, yes, now you will be ready to love and let yourself be loved, to respect and be respected, to admire and be admired.

You will always be accompanied, so you won't look for anyone or anything to fill your moments of solitude. In fact, you may even seek out solitude and silence to be with yourself, have a conversation with yourself, as it's in these moments when you can decide how you want to live your life and who you want to be.

Remember that you don't have much time, so wake up and make the most of it. Make the most of it by being YOU – all of YOU – and living the life you want.

The real-life effects

If you are able to reach this goal of inner connection, the effects on your day-to-day life will be profound. If your partner comes home from work and doesn't tell you about their day or ask you about yours, you'll know that it's okay. You'll understand that they're tired and just don't feel like talking, but from the peace you feel, from the security you feel in being loved and listened to, you'll tell them about your day. You won't wait for them to ask because you won't need constant proof that they love you and that you're important to them. You'll share because you want to ... or not. You may sit in silence on the couch, watching TV and just snuggling, giving them affection, love and understanding in the security of knowing that everything is okay, that they love you and you love them, but right now, you don't feel like talking. And if you want to tell them something and you realise they're not listening, you won't get angry, fearing that it means they don't love you. Perhaps you'll say, 'Hey, listen, something incredible has happened,' and you know what? They will listen.

And if, after a while, from a place of tranquillity, with a body full of love, you decide that you don't really like your partner for whatever reason, you'll leave without resentment, hatred or emptiness, because you'll still have yourself. You might realise that you didn't love them; you loved the possibility of being with someone who loves and protects you. But since you won't have the need for that feeling any more, you'll be much more able to identify whether you truly want to be with that person or not.

You might now be able to say to yourself, *I'm not looking for a partner who loves me, I'm looking for a partner to share all the*

Love

love I have, all the love I am ... I'm looking for a partner I like for who they are, how they speak, how they are with their family and friends, who I like even when we argue ... and I'll give them who I am. I won't wait for them to judge me or approve of me, I'll just be myself, and if they like me and allow a space for me to be my best version of myself, and I like them and allow a space for them to be their best version of themselves, we'll last, because our relationship won't be based on filling emotional voids. I can now fill those on my own.

Once you reach this state, you will be able to think, *I know I'm beautiful. I've told myself that when I've looked in the mirror, and without looking – I know I am. I know I'm not good at certain things, but that's okay. I respect myself, I applaud myself and I encourage myself to keep trying. I don't judge myself for saying that I'm not good. In fact, I don't judge myself for anything. I simply observe and talk about what we can improve, and I don't need anyone to tell me anything.*

You can also ask for advice from people who know more than you about a certain topic, but you'll do it without fear, because you will be open to improving yourself and working towards what you want to be. It will be amazing when someone praises something you've done, but if they don't, that's okay, too. You know very well what's behind what you've done or what you haven't done.

Dare to love

Generally, we are afraid to give love, afraid of being hurt, afraid of being left alone, afraid of loving the wrong person. Perhaps we don't even know how to love. But you know what? Now you know what it feels like to truly feel loved, and now you know that you are capable of giving unconditional love. Remember, you give it to yourself all the time, more and more each day.

Now, you feel like giving love to others as well. You feel like sharing it because you know we all deserve to be loved, to be valued and appreciated, to be understood and heard. And it doesn't depend on any other person, it depends on you – on whether you want to give that love. Once we realise that there are no conditions or rules, we can simply love and value each other and feel compassion for one another, because we can all see ourselves reflected in each other. We understand that we all experience the same feelings, sensations and struggles within ourselves. That each of us lives according to the script that we have written for ourselves as best we can. Who are we to judge anyone's path or reaction?

Whatever you do, whatever happens, you will be loved, so dare to love others the same way. Maybe you can help them realise that they can love themselves and that they deserve it, too. Maybe if they see you without your armour on, they will take theirs off, too, and realise how wonderful life is without it.

And if you still feel like you're not ready to give love to others, then just feel it. Don't focus on giving love to others to help them, just concentrate on feeling it yourself – feeling love, for no particular reason, just for the opportunity to live, for the awareness that your heart beats every day, for the opportunity to be here and have yourself. You don't have to express it if you're not ready yet. I assure you that just wanting to feel it makes the people around you feel inspired to be better by simply witnessing your evolution and the change in your energy. Because your love, even without you realising it, expands from you.

Love

Who are you now?

Once you have removed your armour and faced your fears, ask yourself this: who are you? Do you like yourself? Are you kind? Do you have a sense of humour? Are you beautiful on the inside? How would you now answer that big question from the genie, if it came before you again and asked you what you want? You no longer need external validation – it is not an urgent need, for which you will do whatever it takes – so now you can afford to ask for what you really want. Whatever it is, you will not fail, because in every endeavour you will always encourage yourself, cheer yourself up, accompany yourself and support yourself, so be brave – what do you ask for?

Where do you want to spend the majority of your time? And who with? What job do you want? What does your dream family look like? If you have children, how do you want to raise them? How do you want to be with your friends and family? Remember, you are not alone, whatever happens – if you lose a job, if other people leave you, it's okay ... you are being true, not to your constructed version of yourself with its acquired needs, but to YOURSELF! I'm excited to be here with you, waiting for you to answer this question...

I have rediscovered who I really am several times. In some of the low moments of my life, when fear and uncertainty have overwhelmed me, I have had to take a deep breath and remind myself that I was there for myself. I calmed down ... and suddenly that pressure in my stomach and chest – caused by the fear – went away. In those moments, whatever happens, I know I have myself. I embrace myself, talk to myself, even tell myself jokes if necessary. And I find peace in knowing that together, me and ME, my soul sister, will walk through life supporting each other.

Remember this when, for example, you are with your parents, or your partner, or your children, and they are driving you crazy. Remember that you don't need anything from them; you just want to enjoy them while you have them. Feel tremendous love for them. Breathe and enjoy that they are there with you. Enjoy loving them without asking them to be the way you want them to be, without asking them to give you anything in return. Just love them, with peace and fullness. You no longer need anything from them; you just want them as they are, and you are grateful to life for having them.

Reflection: Practising gratitude

Gratitude is something we can incorporate into the smallest moments on our journey. Anyone you meet on your way can bring something to your life, and guess what? You can also bring something to them.

When you're at the supermarket and it's time to pay, don't think, *Oh, the cashier looks so depressed. Oh, she's so slow, I hope someone else comes to help me.* Instead, be present, say hello and put your things in the bags while thinking about how delicious everything you've bought will be. Don't think, *Oh, I've bought junk food – I'll have to come next time without being hungry. How can I lose weight?* Instead, be grateful for having money to buy food, and for having a supermarket open with so many delicious things in it to buy ... Do you see my point?

Love

Those thoughts are simply the result of fear. Fear that the cashier being slow will make you late getting home. Fear that her bad mood will remind you of how hard life is, when you're trying to stay positive. Fear of gaining weight by eating what you've bought and not being accepted or liked as a result ... At any given time, we harbour a long list of fears that lead us to have constant intrusive thoughts consistent with those fears.

But now we no longer feel fear, and we're not seeking external validation, because we don't need it any more. Instead, we can open ourselves to peace, love and gratitude, and enjoy everything. There will be people who will probably criticise you and say that you've become too naive, that you live in another world. But don't worry, at the same time they will be feeling inspired by you, because that state is what everyone wants to achieve, though few dare to.

And it's not worth cheating, it's not worth pretending, it's not worth judging yourself, thinking, *Oh, I can't do it! I can't enjoy life without thinking about the negative or the problems I have.* When that happens to you, immediately talk to yourself, but without words. Talk to yourself with sensations, and say, 'Calm down, take it slowly, don't torture yourself. You're on the path of trying and only if you continue can you enjoy it. You're doing great, keep going, I'm here.' Or, 'You're doing horribly, but don't worry, it's okay, at least we're laughing and still trying. I'll always be with you – what an adventure!'

You will learn from each person and each situation. Even if they're new, you will be open to getting to know them and exploring them, rather than being afraid of them. And in the meantime, you will be getting to know yourself better, too, because now you're observing yourself, feeling yourself, constantly witnessing how you react and how you are, without judgement.

Now, you are loving yourself. And you are grateful for it!

It all starts with YOU

So that's it, you have the answers now. You can start living for real. You can decide to start approaching life from a different perspective. Now you have YOURSELF. Now you're going to take care of YOURSELF as if you were your own best friend. You're going to love YOURSELF like a mother loves her child. You're going to sustain, support, listen to and accept YOURSELF, with everything you are. You're going to applaud, like and value YOURSELF.

Now you can go back to your daily life with this new love inside you. Go back to work, to your relationships, to your goals, obstacles and successes . . . but not from a place of loneliness, insecurity and fear. Now you can live through all of that, strive for and fulfil your dreams, with all the ups and downs you will encounter along the way, but you will approach it all from your core being – a full, secure, loving, peaceful being.

You can now love everyone and everything, and you can let yourself be loved. You can care, support and nourish yourself and others, without needs, without demands. Go out into the world and then love and live completely! Enjoy life. Squeeze the juice out of every minute of it. Look around you with admiration and gratitude and love all of it.

A powerful side-effect of truly loving yourself is that it gifts you the confidence and energy to take risks, make decisions, express yourself and share yourself. The world needs YOU, YOUR ideas, YOUR opinions and YOUR beautiful love, so allow yourself to rest, work, pause as much as you need, enjoy, cry, laugh and sing . . . because now you're really going to live.

Welcome – and go for it!

Acknowledgements

When I first wrote this book, I kept it hidden on my computer for a couple of years. It was a secret I couldn't bring myself to share – not even with myself. I couldn't quite believe I had written it. Everything changed after a conversation with my friend M.C., who inspired me to embrace my love for writing and my desire to spread a message of authenticity and love. That conversation lit a spark and, little by little, I began opening the cocoon, daring to share my words with others.

The first person I shared the raw manuscript with was my dear friend S.M. She read it with care and gave me her most honest and heartfelt feedback. More than anything, she reminded me that if this book came from my heart, I shouldn't be afraid to share it because there might be people who truly need its message. Her encouragement gave me the courage to keep going. From there, I started rewriting, editing and sharing it with a few more friends whose feedback and inspiration helped me refine the book and, ultimately, prepare it for the world. Every step of the way, I was met with kindness and support, which made this new adventure feel immensely gratifying.

I am especially grateful to Guillem B. who, without hesitation, connected me with David Luxton. After reading the book, David introduced me to my extraordinary literary agent, Jane Graham Maw, who kindly and skillfully guided me through every professional step of this journey. Jane, your advice, expertise and unwavering support have been nothing short of a blessing. To the entire team at Graham Maw Christie Literary Agency, thank you for believing in this project and for everything you've done to bring it to life.

When Lydia G., an amazing editor, believed in my book and wanted to publish it, I could hardly believe it. Lydia, words cannot fully express how grateful I am that Jane brought this book to you and that you embraced it with such enthusiasm. To Lydia, Cyan T., Jane S. and the incredible team at Harper-Collins, thank you for your unwavering support and for making this dream a reality. To Thomas H. and Daniel M., thank you for your expertise and for helping to spread the word about this book.

I feel profoundly blessed by the chain of people who made this book possible. Each one of you played a vital role in this journey, and I will never take for granted the kindness, guidance and encouragement I have received along the way. I am overjoyed and immensely grateful that I finally dared to write and publish my first book. And that I found the perfect people to help me bring it to life.

Thank you all – this has been an extraordinary journey, and I cannot wait to see what comes next.